T0179976

Praise for *The "I Don't Want to Cook" Book: Dinners Done in One Pot*

"Alyssa Brantley not only makes meal planning a breeze but also inspires with practical tips to maximize flavor. This guide is the perfect companion for anyone seeking nutritious, flavorful meals without the hassle."

—CHIHYU SMITH,
Creator of *I Heart Umami* and author of *Asian Paleo*

"Alyssa hit a home run with this beautiful cookbook! It is a dream come true for busy individuals looking for nourishing meals that are ready in a jiffy with low fuss and little cleanup! If you find cooking to be intimidating or overwhelming, Alyssa's helpful tips make cooking approachable to anyone of any skill level."

—JULIA MUELLER,
Cookbook author and founder of TheRoastedRoot.net

"Finding recipes that are delicious, easy to make, family friendly, AND full of nutrient-dense ingredients can feel a bit like chasing a unicorn. Yet Alyssa always seems to tick all those boxes with her recipes. This cookbook is a kitchen must-have for busy families!"

—TAESHA BUTLER,
Creator of *The Natural Nurturer*

Praise for *The "I Don't Want to Cook" Book: Dinners Done in One Pot*

"Alyssa makes dinner one (pot!) and done for those of us who can't handle piles of plates at the end of a long day. This book makes life easier—and tastier—for dinner makers everywhere!"

—JENNIFER ROBINS,
Founder of Legit Bread Company and cookbook author

"Prepare to be amazed once again by Alyssa Brantley's culinary brilliance! These dishes will help home cooks get dinner on the table without all the fuss—or the mountain of dishes!"

—KARISTA BENNETT,
Author of *For the Love of Seafood* and *The Oregon Farm Table Cookbook*

THE "I DON'T WANT TO COOK" BOOK:

DINNERS DONE IN ONE POT

100 LOW-PREP,
NO-MESS RECIPES
for Your Skillet, Sheet Pan,
Pressure Cooker, and More!

ALYSSA BRANTLEY
FOUNDER OF EVERYDAYMAVEN

ADAMS MEDIA

New York London Toronto Sydney New Delhi

Adams Media
An Imprint of Simon & Schuster, LLC
100 Technology Center Drive
Stoughton, Massachusetts 02072

First Adams Media hardcover edition October 2024

ADAMS MEDIA and colophon are registered trademarks of Simon & Schuster, LLC.

Simon & Schuster: Celebrating 100 Years of Publishing in 2024

For information about special discounts for bulk purchases, please contact Simon & Schuster Special Sales at 1-866-506-1949 or business@simonandschuster.com.

The Simon & Schuster Speakers Bureau can bring authors to your live event. For more information or to book an event, contact the Simon & Schuster Speakers Bureau at 1-866-248-3049 or visit our website at www.simonspeakers.com.

Interior design, illustrations, and hand lettering by Priscilla Yuen
Photographs by Emily Weeks
Interior images © 123RF/lekstuntkite, kwangmoo, Oxana Lebedeva

Manufactured in China

10 9 8 7 6 5 4 3 2 1

Library of Congress Cataloging-in-Publication Data
Names: Brantley, Alyssa, author.
Title: The "I don't want to cook" book: dinners done in one pot / Alyssa Brantley, founder of EverydayMaven.
Other titles: "I do not want to cook" book: dinners done in one pot
Description: First Adams Media hardcover edition. | Stoughton, Massachusetts: Adams Media, 2024. | Series: I don't want to cook series | Includes index.
Identifiers: LCCN 2024011057 | ISBN 9781507222577 (hc) | ISBN 9781507222584 (ebook)
Subjects: LCSH: Quick and easy cooking. | One-dish meals. | Smart cookers. | LCGFT: Cookbooks.
Classification: LCC TX833.5 .B69 2024 | DDC 641.5/12--dc23/eng/20240314
LC record available at https://lccn.loc.gov/2024011057

ISBN 978-1-5072-2257-7
ISBN 978-1-5072-2258-4 (ebook)

For my two greatest creations: Deacon and Vaughn.
And to my husband: Kareem, you are my everything.

CONTENTS

2 SIZZLING SKILLET CREATIONS / 29

3 DUTCH OVEN DINNERS / 51

4

DINNERS IN A MIXING BOWL / 71

5

CONVENIENT CASSEROLES / 85

10 WEEKNIGHT WOK WINS / 177

11 DUMP AND GO SLOW COOKER MEALS / 193

INTRO

Do busy schedules make it difficult to plan—not to mention cook—dinner? Would you rather spend more time having fun with family or checking something off your to-do list than washing mountains of dishes after a meal? Tired of rotating the same five dishes every week?

When you find yourself staring into the refrigerator after a long day, wishing for a magic solution to put a satisfying dinner on the table in record time and with minimal cleanup, *The "I Don't Want to Cook" Book: Dinners Done in One Pot* is here to help! In Chapter 1, you'll learn more about what makes one pot cooking so much easier than other methods, as well as shortcuts to even faster meals. You'll also discover the different pots (and pans and other vessels) used in the recipes that follow, along with helpful information for caring for and using them.

Then, in the following chapters, you'll find one hundred delectable dinners that effortlessly come together. All of the recipes are organized according to what that dish is cooked in. From sizzling stir-fries to hearty casseroles, these meals include:

DUCTION

- Delicious skillet dishes like Italian Sausage and White Bean Skillet with Tortellini (Chapter 2)
- Dutch oven delights like Turkey Potpie with Biscuit Crust (Chapter 3)
- Satisfying casseroles like Vegetarian Pesto Lazy Lasagna (Chapter 5)
- Simple sheet pan medleys like Sheet Pan Shrimp Scampi with Broccoli and Garlic Bread (Chapter 6)
- Comforting soups like Old Bay Corn Chowder with Pancetta (Chapter 9)
- And more!

If you know how much time you have to spare in the kitchen, you can also flip to the appendix in the back of this book to choose a recipe that fits your schedule. Here, the recipes are organized from shortest to longest total cook and prep times.

Gone are the days of elaborate prep, numerous pots and pans, and complex recipes! With *The "I Don't Want to Cook" Book: Dinners Done in One Pot*, you'll embrace the simplicity and efficiency of one pot cooking. Whether you're busy juggling work and family commitments, seeking convenience without compromising on taste, or just don't want to cook, this cookbook is your invitation to indulge in mouthwatering creations while reclaiming your evenings.

CHAPTER ONE

QUICK, EASY, AND DELICIOUS ONE POT COOKING

Welcome to a world where making dinner is no longer stressful, where prep work is as minimal as possible, where cleanup doesn't take forever, and where the homemade dinners you prepare are not only easy but also delicious. When you combine the tips and tools in this chapter with the recipes later in this book, you are well on your way to a tasty and *fast* future in the kitchen.

Everyone has days when they just don't want to cook. Or maybe you never have the time or energy to think about (much less make) dinner. This chapter is here to help. In the pages that follow, you will find everything you need for successful one pot cooking, including information and care tips for the different "pots" (or pans, skillets, dishes, etc.) used in this book, the two most important steps any cook should follow, and helpful shortcuts such as using prechopped and frozen vegetables. The nights spent toiling away at dinner and cleaning up after the chaos are over.

The Two Most Important One Pot Cooking Tips

Before jumping into the tips and tools for one pot cooking, there are a couple secrets every home cook should know. The two most important tips to always follow in order to save time and energy in the kitchen are:

1 **Always read through the entire recipe before starting.** This means reading through the ingredient list, the cooking instructions, and the notes or tips if they are listed. Make sure that you understand the recipe and have the ingredients and tools needed to execute it. Don't just scan the ingredients and get started—reading the instructions in full before you start *will save you time*!

2 **Prep *before* you begin cooking, not during!** This is arguably the most important cooking habit to get into. Especially since so many of the recipes in this book move quickly. The goal is to get you in and out of the kitchen as fast as possible. While you might not want to spend the time crushing garlic, measuring spices, and organizing your ingredients before you start cooking, prepping *before cooking* actually saves you time in the long run. This is a guaranteed way to avoid missing an ingredient or step along the way—or even worse, burning or overcooking something while you frantically try to grab that missing ingredient.

Thoroughly reading the recipe will be your first step in the kitchen, and prepping will be the second. The prep work will also include making sure you have the right pot (or other cooking vessel) ready for the recipe at hand. In the next section, you will learn about each of the different vessels used in the recipes in this book.

One Pot, One Pan, One Vessel

Each recipe in the following chapters uses just one pot, pan, dish, or other vessel to cook up a delicious meal. In this section, you will learn more about the different vessels used, including any important safety or cleaning tips, so you will be ready with the necessary tools when you begin making recipes.

12" or 14" Cast Iron Skillet

The cast iron skillet is an everyday workhorse. Very affordable, a well-cared-for cast iron skillet will not only last forever, but actually get better with age and use. Make delicious dinners in no time like Old Bay Surf and Turf with Snap Peas, Quick Beef Enchilada Skillet, Lemon Dijon Chicken with Orzo and Peas, and more.

Always preheat your cast iron skillet over medium heat for 2–3 minutes before adding any cooking fat. You don't want the skillet to get to the point where it is smoking or you could scorch your cooking fat or burn your food.

After cooking with your cast iron skillet, rinse it with hot water, then dry thoroughly. If there are stuck-on food bits, use a scrub brush to remove them before drying. Avoid soaking, or using abrasive cleaning powders or dish soap. Another option for cleaning is to make a quick paste of 1 tablespoon kosher salt and 1 tablespoon avocado oil (or other high-heat cooking oil) and use it to dislodge anything stuck to the skillet. Then rinse and dry.

If the skillet looks dry or like the patina (the shiny coating that develops over time, which makes the skillet nonstick) needs to be refreshed, warm it up over medium heat for a few minutes. Once dry and hot, reduce heat to low and add a small amount (approximately ¼ teaspoon to ½ teaspoon depending on how dry the skillet is) of avocado oil (or other high-heat cooking oil). Use a paper towel to rub the oil into the skillet, focusing on the cooking surface but giving the sides, bottom, and handle a quick swipe, and take care not to leave any oil pooling. You want the thinnest layer possible. Turn the heat off and let the skillet sit on the warm burner until completely cool, about 30–45 minutes.

Always be careful when transferring a hot cast iron skillet from stovetop to oven and use two oven-safe gloves with a good grip. And, to serve food directly out of a hot cast iron skillet, be sure to use a heat-safe trivet on your table and avoid touching the handle. You can always lay a doubled or tripled folded kitchen towel over the hot handle as a reminder not to touch it.

5.5-Quart or Larger Dutch Oven (Round Preferred)

The Dutch oven is one of the most versatile cooking vessels, and can be used for a variety of cooking methods. You will find that the Chapter 3: Dutch Oven Dinners recipes in this book mainly use the Dutch oven for stovetop cooking, like Creamy Pesto Pasta with Salami, or start on the stovetop to develop flavor or brown ingredients and then are quickly transferred to the oven to bake for the majority of the cooking time, such as Turkey Potpie with Biscuit Crust and Dutch Oven Beef and Bean Tamale Pie.

Dutch ovens are typically made of cast iron but covered in an enamel coating. They usually have thick walls and a heavy oven-safe lid. Some of the more commonly available brands include Le Creuset, Staub, Lodge, and Ikea. The key is to look for as high quality a one as your budget allows so that it will last for a long time without the enamel coating chipping or getting damaged.

It is not recommended to use metal or sharp tools when cooking with a Dutch oven as you can damage the enamel coating, so stick with wood, silicone, and high-heat-safe plastic tools.

Always preheat your Dutch oven for a few minutes before adding any cooking fat or ingredients, especially if you're searing or browning, as this helps to ensure even cooking and prevent sticking.

Finally, always allow your Dutch oven to cool before cleaning. Avoid abrasive tools and powders that could damage the enamel. For stuck-on food bits, soak the Dutch oven in warm, soapy water and use a gentle sponge to clean.

Large Stainless Steel Mixing Bowl

It's always a great idea to have a set of at least three different-sized metal mixing bowls. For most of the recipes in Chapter 4: Dinners in a Mixing Bowl, you will need a large stainless steel mixing bowl. And when it comes to mixing bowls, bigger is always better! The more room you have to toss a salad or noodles, the easier it is to manage and the less splatter or cleanup you have to deal with.

You will find that the mixing bowl dinner recipes are some of the quickest in this book. None have any active or hands-on cooking time. There is not actually any "cooking," just prep time ranging from 5 minutes (for the Speedy Pesto Salmon and White Bean Lettuce Wraps) to 15 minutes (for the Chopped Italian Sub Bowl).

The recipes optimize for less cleanup by combining dressing or sauce at the beginning of the recipe where possible to avoid having to use a separate bowl. In keeping with the less-is-more theme, serve your meal right from the mixing bowl and, if it's dishwasher safe, toss it in the dishwasher.

9" × 13" (3-Quart) Rectangular Casserole Dish

The word "casserole" usually refers to both the cooking vessel and the type of food cooked in it. It's recommended to use a 9" × 13" (3-quart) rectangular casserole dish, but any shape 3-quart casserole dish can be safely substituted. All of the casserole recipes in this book are made in a casserole dish made of glass (like Pyrex), ceramic, or earthenware. While there are some metal casserole dishes on the market, they are not recommended as they tend to function more like roasting pans and can have uneven hot spots.

You will find that all of the casserole recipes in Chapter 5: Convenient Casseroles just need to be assembled and then put into the oven—no precooking, sautéing, or searing. If the recipe includes rice, noodles, uncooked chicken, or crumbled sausage, it's cooked directly in the casserole!

These modern casseroles are made with whole-food ingredients. Forget processed seasoning packets or mushy vegetables and leftovers together with jarred soup. You will find inventive dinners like Deconstructed Chicken Cordon Bleu Casserole and twists on classic favorites like Meatloaf Casserole with Tater Tot Topping.

In the case that your casserole dish has a large amount of stuck-on food bits, add a squirt or two of dish soap and hot water and leave it to soak for an hour or so before handwashing. While most casserole dishes are dishwasher safe, always check cleaning instructions before placing in the dishwasher as some may require top rack cleaning only or not be suitable for the dishwasher. It's recommended to give the casserole dish a once-over with a kitchen sponge to remove any food bits before placing in a dishwasher.

18" × 13" Rimmed Sheet Pan

When it comes to cooking an entire dinner on a sheet pan (also called a baking sheet), there are a couple things that really make a difference. First, it's recommended to always use a rimmed sheet pan to prevent juices or ingredients from spilling. A rimmed sheet pan also makes it much easier to prep ingredients directly on the sheet pan and to flip during cooking, like in the Spicy Sausage with Cabbage Wedges and Butter Potatoes.

When cooking with a sheet pan, always preheat the oven. Most oven preheat cycles are between 8 and 10 minutes—use that time to do the prep work for the recipe.

High-quality sheet pans are affordable and last for a long time. There are many different types of sheet pans or baking sheets. For the recipes in this book, heavy-duty, rimmed aluminum sheet pans are recommended, as they are a bit thicker and more robust than standard sheet pans (which are typically used for baking). Heavy-duty aluminum sheet pans are less prone to warping, are excellent for high-heat cooking, and have a longer life.

Stainless steel sheet pans tend to be heavier than aluminum, take a bit longer to heat up, and can be more difficult to clean. Nonstick sheet pans are not recommended for the following recipes, as they are not meant for high-heat cooking and are not as durable as they require gentle handling to preserve the nonstick coating. Insulated sheet pans usually have an air layer between two metal layers. While this helps to distribute heat more evenly, they are mostly meant for delicate baked goods to prevent browning and make it difficult to get the desired browning and crispy edges.

When it's appropriate for the recipe, parchment paper is recommended to line the sheet pan in order to minimize cleanup. You can also use a Silpat.

Handwashing is recommended for heavy-duty aluminum sheet pans. For stuck-on food bits, add a squirt or two of dish soap and hot water. Allow to soak for at least an hour and continue cleaning with a kitchen sponge. It's not recommended to place aluminum sheet pans in the dishwasher.

Gas Grill

Depending on where you live, you may be a year-round griller, a seasonal griller, or a weather-dependent griller. Whichever it is, Chapter 7: Family Grill Nights has you covered with easy dinners like Taco Salmon with Avocado Lime Mash and Grilled Tomatoes or Grilled Flank Steak with Summer Squash and Pesto Toast.

It's always recommended to preheat your gas grill for at least 10 minutes to burn off any food residue from your last grilling session. This also ensures that the grates are hot enough for proper searing and helps prevent sticking.

Another trick is to oil the grates right before placing food on them. For this reason, it's recommended to use a paper towel or basting brush to quickly apply some high-heat cooking oil, such as avocado oil, to the grates right before placing the food. If you oil the grates too early, the oil can burn off.

As tempting as it can be, don't skip quickly cleaning the grill after each use. For gas grills, it's recommended to turn all of the burners to the highest heat setting, close the lid, and let the grill heat for 5–6 minutes. Turn off, open lid, and allow grill to cool for 30–45 minutes before using a brush or scraper to remove loosened food debris. If you are using a wire brush, always use a moist rag or wet paper towels to wipe the grill grates after cleaning to ensure that no brush wires are left behind. This type of quick cleaning helps to prevent the buildup of grease and food residue. And it ensures much-better-tasting food! It's not recommended to cook the recipes in this book over an open flame grill with coals or fire.

6-Quart Instant Pot®

The Instant Pot® is an electric pressure cooker that cooks two to six times faster than conventional cooking methods. And, because you can sauté or sear directly in the pot before cooking under pressure, the Instant Pot® allows you to quickly and easily build layers of flavor in a dish. Using the Instant Pot®, you can make sumptuous flavor-packed dinners in record time using tougher proteins that would take all day to tenderize in the oven, like Hands-Off Homemade French Dip Sandwiches, Lamb Korma with Potatoes and Peas, and even Quick and Easy Pork Posole with Shredded Cabbage.

When you select the pressure setting and set the cooking time, the Instant Pot® will still need to "reach pressure" before it begins cooking. For this reason, an approximate "time to pressure" number is included in each of the Chapter 8: Instant Dinners recipes' hands-off cooking time, in addition to any other hands-off cooking time so that you can more accurately plan your time.

There are two main ways to relieve pressure on the Instant Pot® when the cooking time is up: quick release and natural release. Quick release is where you depress the pressure valve as soon as cooking time is up. Make sure to have the Instant Pot® on a stable surface and turn the Instant Pot® so that the valve doesn't spray on your cabinets, or any other items you don't want to get steamy. It is not recommended to cover the valve with a towel but it is advisable to place a kitchen towel on the counter behind the valve to capture any steam or droplets to make cleanup quicker.

With a natural pressure release, the Instant Pot® switches to warming mode and pressure begins to naturally release slowly. Sometimes you will see natural pressure release for a specific amount of time, such as "let pressure release naturally for 15 minutes, then quick-release remaining steam."

When switching from the Sauté mode to the Manual or Pressure Cook mode, always make sure to scrape the bottom of the pot for any stuck food or browned bits to avoid getting a "burn" warning, which will shut off the pot.

It's important to remember that while the new electric pressure cookers are much safer than their predecessors, you should never try to force open an Instant Pot®. The pressure must be fully released and the pressure valve must fall before the lid can be removed. Always make sure your arm or hand is not over the vent when opening the pressure valve. Some people prefer to use a wooden spoon or tongs to open the pressure valve.

If your Instant Pot® is not coming to pressure properly, it's usually because the sealing ring isn't secured properly. Or the vent isn't set to sealing. Check for these possible causes first, then consult the troubleshooting section of the user manual.

The stainless steel insert of the Instant Pot® is easy to clean with a kitchen sponge and hot soapy water or can even be placed into the dishwasher (bottom or top rack).

6-Quart or Larger Soup Pot

It's recommended to use a stainless steel soup pot that holds at least 6 quarts. For the recipes in Chapter 9: Soup Pot Suppers, a larger soup pot won't make a material difference; however, a smaller pot could overflow. Stainless steel soup pots are preferred, as they are durable, easy to clean, and nonreactive. Look for a pot with sturdy handles and a tight-fitting lid. A 6-quart or larger Dutch oven can be substituted for a soup pot.

In Chapter 9, you will find substantial dinner soups filled with flavor and texture like Turmeric Chicken and Rice Soup, a meal in a bowl that is on the table in around 40 minutes, with most of that being hands-off cooking time. You will also find thick and chunky stew recipes, one pot pasta dinners, and even 20-Minute Steamed Mussels with Buttered Peas.

Most soup pots can be easily cleaned with hot water and a soapy kitchen sponge, but check manufacturer directions prior to first use to see if your soup pot has any special instructions. For stuck-on food bits, soak with a squirt or two of dish soap and hot water for at least an hour before cleaning with a sponge.

14" or Larger Flat Bottom Carbon Steel Wok

A wok is a Cantonese cooking pot. It's recommended to get a 14" or larger carbon steel wok with a flat bottom as the material is lightweight and heats very quickly.

Woks generally come with round or flat bottoms. While a round bottom is more traditional, a flat bottom works better with all types of cooking surfaces such as gas, electric, and induction. If you have gas or open-fire cooking and prefer a round wok, make sure to purchase a "wok ring," which is a circular metal device with open sides that stabilizes the wok for cooking.

Nonstick or enamel-lined woks are not recommended as they are not meant for high-temperature cooking. All of the recipes in Chapter 10: Weeknight Wok Wins are cooked over high heat. You will find quick-cooking and delicious wok dinners like Super Quick Beef and Broccoli, Honey Soy Chicken Thighs with Snow Peas, and even a 15-Minute Coconut Curry Noodle Soup with Shrimp. A stainless steel wok can work, but you will usually need to use more oil than called for as the surfaces are prone to sticking. Cast iron woks are really heavy and cumbersome and can be dangerous when filled with food.

Carbon steel woks need to be washed, dried, and re-seasoned after each use, similar to cast iron skillets. Refer to the cleaning tips in the 12" or 14" Cast Iron Skillet section.

6-Quart or Larger Slow Cooker

While there are many different types of slow cookers on the market, for the purposes of the recipes in Chapter 11: Dump and Go Slow Cooker Meals, all you need is a 6-quart or larger oval slow cooker with an insert that doesn't have any other functionality except cooking on either low or high heat and keeping warm until you turn it off. You will be able to effortlessly create delicious dinners like Red Beans and Rice with Smoked Sausage (no presoaking of the beans necessary), Hoisin Pulled Pork Rice Bowls with Cucumbers, and Mississippi-Style Pot Roast Sandwiches with a filling that can be served in a hearty sandwich or as a platter.

There are many choices for slow cooker insert materials, including stoneware or ceramic, aluminum, nonstick, oven-safe inserts, and even glass. Stoneware or ceramic are recommended as they provide even heat distribution, retain heat well, and are very durable for cleaning.

If the recipe instructions don't include a variation to cook on high as an option, then it's not recommended to modify the cooking time.

Resist the temptation to lift the lid and stir around the contents of the slow cooker while cooking, unless expressly called for in the recipe, as this can dramatically reduce the cooking temperature and release needed moisture.

Slow cooker inserts can easily be cleaned with hot water and a soapy sponge. For stuck-on food bits, soak with a squirt or two of dish soap and hot water for at least an hour before continuing to clean. As the inserts are on the large side, it is not usually recommended to place them in the dishwasher.

Additional Tools for One Pot Cooking

While everything you make in the following chapters will be cooked in one vessel, a dish may call for chopping ingredients, whipping up a simple dressing, measuring an ingredient, etc. For these steps, you will also want to have a few additional tools on hand:

- Knives (including chefs knife, paring knife, and serrated edge knife)
- Cutting board
- Small mixing bowl
- 2-cup glass measuring cup with handle (such as Pyrex or Anchor Hocking)
- Set each of measuring spoons and measuring cups
- Digital food scale
- Garlic press
- Large colander

- Spatula(s)
- Wooden spoon(s)
- Whisk
- Tongs
- Instant-read thermometer
- Can opener
- Microplane or handheld grater
- High-heat oven mitts for oven and grill
- Grill tools (long-handled tongs, flipper, grill brush)

Again, the recipes in this book have been made with convenience in mind, so many involve mixing ingredients straight in the cooking vessel or using premeasured packages. The need for these additional tools is kept as minimal as possible, and cleanup is just a quick wash with soap and warm water.

Shortcuts for Easier One Pot Cooking

Every recipe in the following chapters is made with your time and effort in mind, and that includes using a number of helpful shortcuts. In this section, you will explore simple ways to make one pot cooking as easy and fast as possible.

Convenience Vegetables

Convenience vegetables are pre-prepped, ready to use, convenient, and time-saving. You will find many recipes in this book that call for shredded cabbage, shredded iceberg lettuce, cleaned and trimmed green beans, washed fresh baby spinach, and fresh broccoli and cauliflower florets. Look for these items in the produce department at your grocery store. Many stores carry organic versions as well if preferred.

Many recipes call for an onion, but dicing an onion can be time-consuming, so in every single recipe where it is possible, a much quicker preparation of onion is used: Halve it, peel it, place the flat side down, and thinly slice. There are a few recipes where diced onion makes a difference, however. In these cases, to save time, scope out the convenience vegetable section for containers or bags of already diced onion.

And to make quick work of fresh garlic, most recipes in this book call for crushed garlic, which is prepped using a garlic press. To save even more time, look in the convenience vegetable section for already peeled whole garlic cloves. It is not recommended to use jarred, chopped garlic or frozen garlic cubes as both have additives that dramatically change the flavor and will impact the final result.

These recipes save even more time by focusing on whole food–based pantry convenience items like canned beans, canned tomatoes, high-quality marinara sauce, olives, and marinated artichokes.

Frozen vegetables are another staple you will want to take advantage of. They are often cheaper and sometimes even more nutritious since they are flash frozen to preserve freshness!

Precooked Rice

A fair number of recipes call for reheated precooked rice. Look in the grocery store freezer section for bags of already cooked white or brown rice and stock your freezer. A more affordable option is to batch-cook rice once a month or so, let it cool, and pack it in freezer-safe storage bags for future meals. Well-packaged rice should last for up to six months in the freezer.

Fast Proteins

You will find that many of the recipes feature quick-cooking, hassle-free proteins like boneless, skinless chicken thighs or breast, ground beef, cubed stew meat, whole roasts, bulk sausage (this means loose sausage out of the casing), fresh or frozen peeled and deveined shrimp, and rotisserie chicken. (If you can only find uncooked sausage in the casing, just use a paring knife to slice open the casing and transfer to a bowl.) Many stores sell packages of already shredded or cubed rotisserie chicken. If you can't find this, it's recommended to buy a couple rotisserie chickens during your food shopping trip and pull the meat off as soon as you get home. Then freeze in 1-pound portions. These are all considered "shortcut meats," or proteins that not only cook quickly but don't need a lot of prep work. These well-packaged frozen portions should last for up to four months in the freezer.

Cooking in One Pot

One pot cooking is your answer to having more home-cooked meals to share with family and friends while spending less time shopping, prepping, and cleaning. And with the information and tools in this chapter, you're ready to start whipping up some delicious one pot recipes. Have your own tricks for making cooking faster and easier? Feel free to use any smart supermarket shortcuts, omit garnishes as much as possible, skip the ingredients and steps that you find too fussy or unnecessary, and not feel bad about it. Let's get cooking!

CHAPTER TWO

SIZZLING SKILLET CREATIONS

29

Welcome to the tasty world of cast iron skillet dinners! In this chapter, you will explore a wide range of one pan dinner recipes that are not only delicious but also easy to prepare using your trusty 12" or 14" cast iron skillet.

Whip up inventive but easy meals like the Pierogi, Andouille Sausage, and Onion Skillet that uses pierogies right from the freezer; Shortcut Blackened Shrimp with Grits and Greens that tastes like a restaurant dish; and Old Bay Surf and Turf with Snap Peas in just one skillet in around 25 minutes! While all of the recipes in this chapter are developed for a 12" or 14" cast iron skillet, a 12" or 14" oven-safe stainless steel frying pan can be substituted. Just keep in mind that you may need to add additional fat to the pan first to prevent sticking.

Broken Linguine with Clams

SERVES 4

Create a restaurant-worthy version of linguine with clams at home by using high-quality canned clams, dry white wine, and a handful of other easy-to-find ingredients. Cook the pasta right in the skillet and create the sauce in just minutes while the pasta drains. The entire dish comes together in less than 20 minutes of active cook time!

PREP TIME: 8 MINUTES • ACTIVE COOK TIME: 16 MINUTES • HANDS-OFF COOK TIME: N/A

1 tablespoon kosher salt

1 pound uncooked linguine pasta, cracked in half

1 cup reserved pasta cooking liquid

6 tablespoons salted butter, divided

4 cloves garlic, peeled and crushed

1/2 teaspoon ground black pepper

1/4 teaspoon crushed red pepper flakes

1 cup dry white wine

2 (6.5-ounce) cans chopped clams with juice

1/4 cup finely chopped fresh flat-leaf parsley

1 Add 2" of cold water to a 12" or larger cast iron skillet, then add salt, set over high heat, and bring to a rolling boil.

2 Once boiling, add linguine and cook 2 minutes less than package instructions indicate (about 6 1/2–7 minutes). Reserve 1 cup of pasta cooking water, then drain pasta into a colander, discarding remaining cooking water.

3 Return skillet to medium heat and add 4 tablespoons butter. Once melted, add garlic, black pepper, and red pepper flakes, stirring continuously, 45 seconds or until garlic is fragrant.

4 Increase heat to high, add wine, and cook 1 minute. Add clams with their juice. Bring to a boil, reduce heat to medium, and reduce sauce for 2 minutes.

Continued ▶

5 Return drained pasta to skillet and use tongs to toss until pasta finishes cooking and absorbs about half of the sauce, approximately 1½ minutes. Stir in remaining 2 tablespoons butter and 2–4 tablespoons of pasta cooking water (depending on how much liquid has cooked off) until sauce is slightly thicker, about 1 minute.

6 Remove from heat, divide onto four plates, and top each plate with 1 tablespoon parsley. Serve immediately.

PER SERVING
Calories: 620 | Fat: 20g | Protein: 20g | Sodium: 1,064mg | Fiber: 4g | Carbohydrates: 90g | Sugar: 4g

Tips, Substitutions, and More...

Bottled all-natural clam juice can be substituted for the white wine if preferred. For an extra kick of heat, add additional crushed red pepper flakes along with the chopped parsley right before serving.

Creamy Sun-Dried Tomato, Shrimp, and Gnocchi Skillet

SERVES 4

This 15-minute flavor-packed skillet dinner combines quick-cooking shelf-stable potato gnocchi with the convenience of already peeled and deveined shrimp. Add a few key seasonings, sun-dried tomatoes in oil, and just enough heavy cream to create a magical sauce that will have you licking your plate clean.

PREP TIME: 7 MINUTES • ACTIVE COOK TIME: 8 MINUTES • HANDS-OFF COOK TIME: N/A

2 tablespoons salted butter

1 1/2 pounds uncooked, peeled, deveined large shrimp, fresh or defrosted and drained

1 teaspoon kosher salt, divided

1/2 teaspoon Italian seasoning

1/4 teaspoon ground black pepper

1/4 cup sun-dried tomatoes in oil, roughly chopped

2 tablespoons sun-dried tomato oil

6 cloves garlic, peeled and crushed

1 pound shelf-stable vacuum-packed potato gnocchi

1 cup low-sodium chicken broth, divided

1 (5-ounce) bag fresh baby spinach

1/4 cup heavy cream

1/4 teaspoon crushed red pepper flakes

1 Heat a 12" or larger cast iron skillet over medium-high heat. Once hot, add butter, shrimp, 1/2 teaspoon salt, Italian seasoning, and black pepper. Cook shrimp 45 seconds per side. Use tongs to remove shrimp to a dinner plate and set aside.

2 Add sun-dried tomatoes, sun-dried tomato oil, and garlic to skillet; sauté 30 seconds, stirring constantly. Add gnocchi and 1/2 cup broth. Cook 2 minutes, stirring frequently.

3 Add spinach and remaining 1/2 cup broth and cook 2 more minutes, stirring frequently to help spinach wilt and sauce thicken. Stir in cooked shrimp, heavy cream, red pepper flakes, and remaining 1/2 teaspoon salt. Continue cooking 1 minute, stirring constantly, for the sauce to thicken.

4 Remove from heat and serve immediately.

PER SERVING
Calories: 545 | Fat: 21g | Protein: 41g | Sodium: 876mg | Fiber: 3g | Carbohydrates: 48g | Sugar: 2g

Shortcut Blackened Shrimp with Grits and Greens

SERVES 4

Create creamy homemade grits topped with blackened shrimp and sautéed spinach in under 20 minutes of active prep and active cooking time. Transfer the cast iron skillet to the oven to finish cooking for just 12 minutes and enjoy a wonderful one pot dinner in no time.

PREP TIME: 8 MINUTES • ACTIVE COOK TIME: 10 MINUTES • HANDS-OFF COOK TIME: 12 MINUTES

1 pound uncooked, peeled, deveined large shrimp, tails off, fresh or defrosted and drained

2 tablespoons extra-virgin olive oil

2 tablespoons blackening seasoning

2 tablespoons salted butter

1 medium yellow onion, peeled and finely chopped

1 (5-ounce) bag fresh baby spinach

3 cups low-sodium chicken broth

1 cup heavy cream

1 1/2 teaspoons Frank's RedHot Original Cayenne Pepper Sauce

1/2 teaspoon kosher salt

1 cup stone-ground grits

1 cup shredded Cheddar cheese

1. Preheat oven to 375°F.

2. In a small bowl or on a cutting board, toss shrimp with oil and blackening seasoning. Set aside.

3. Heat a 12" or larger cast iron skillet over medium-high heat. Once hot, add butter, then onion and spinach. Sauté 3 minutes, stirring occasionally, or until spinach is wilted and onions begin to soften. Transfer to a dinner plate or bowl and set aside.

4. Keeping heat set to medium-high, add broth, heavy cream, hot sauce, and salt to skillet. Stir to combine and bring to a boil. Once boiling, add grits, reduce heat to medium-low to simmer, and whisk continuously 5 minutes or until grits thicken.

5. Turn off heat and stir in cheese. Arrange shrimp in a circular pattern, pushing down each slightly into the grits. Add onion and spinach mixture, spreading out in a single layer over shrimp and grits.

6. Bake on center rack 12 minutes or until shrimp are cooked through. Remove and rest 5 minutes, then serve.

PER SERVING
Calories: 555 | Fat: 40g | Protein: 33g | Sodium: 533mg | Fiber: 3g | Carbohydrates: 15g | Sugar: 9g

Avocado Black Bean Quesadillas with Spicy Jack Cheese

SERVES 4

These quick and easy skillet quesadillas are loaded with flavor and texture. A delicious vegetarian meal ready in just 20 minutes. If you have full-fat sour cream or plain Greek yogurt on hand, add a scoop mixed with jarred salsa to the side for a delicious dipping sauce. To add even more vegetables, serve alongside a handful of sliced cucumber or celery.

PREP TIME: 8 MINUTES ● ACTIVE COOK TIME: 12 MINUTES ● HANDS-OFF COOK TIME: N/A

4 (10") flour tortillas

4 ounces shredded pepper jack cheese, divided

1 (15-ounce) can black beans, drained and rinsed

1 teaspoon taco seasoning

1/2 teaspoon kosher salt (*only if taco seasoning is salt-free)

1 large avocado, peeled, pitted, and diced

1/4 cup baby arugula

16 pickled jalapeño slices

1 Place tortillas on a cutting board or on the kitchen counter. Sprinkle only one side (so that you can fold it) of each tortilla with 1/2 ounce cheese and 1/4 of each remaining ingredient. Divide up remaining 2 ounces cheese and sprinkle atop the filling.

2 Fold each quesadilla in half and gently press down so that each looks like a half circle.

3 Heat a 12" or larger cast iron skillet over medium heat 2–3 minutes until hot.

4 Place two quesadillas at a time in the skillet and cook 3 minutes, pressing gently with a spatula one or two times during cooking to "seal" the quesadilla as the cheese melts. Flip and repeat cooking 3 minutes. Transfer to large serving plates and repeat with remaining quesadillas.

5 Cut each quesadilla into four triangles and serve.

PER SERVING
Calories: 747 | Fat: 30g | Protein: 21g | Sodium: 1,351mg | Fiber: 12g | Carbohydrates: 93g | Sugar: 7g

Old Bay Surf and Turf with Snap Peas

SERVES
4

While Old Bay seasoning is traditionally thought of as a seafood seasoning, it also makes a flavorful spice rub for steak. This quick one pan surf and turf is made with only six ingredients and ready in just 25 minutes total, but feels like a fancy dinner!

PREP TIME: 5 MINUTES ● ACTIVE COOK TIME: 12 MINUTES ● HANDS-OFF COOK TIME: 8 MINUTES

1½ pounds (1"-thick) boneless New York strip steak, patted dry

1 pound uncooked, peeled, deveined large shrimp, fresh or defrosted and drained, patted dry

3 tablespoons avocado oil, divided

3 tablespoons Old Bay seasoning, divided

1 pound snap peas

1 tablespoon salted butter

1 Preheat oven to 350°F.

2 While oven is preheating, place steak and shrimp on a cutting board or dinner plate and rub both sides of the steak with 1 tablespoon oil and 2 tablespoons Old Bay seasoning until well coated. Toss shrimp with 1 tablespoon oil and remaining 1 tablespoon Old Bay seasoning until well coated.

3 Heat a 12" or larger cast iron skillet over medium-high heat (closer to high). Once hot, add remaining 1 tablespoon oil and then seasoned steak. Cook undisturbed 2½ minutes.

4 Flip steak and cook on the other side an additional 2½ minutes. Turn off stovetop heat and transfer skillet to center rack of oven. Bake 8 minutes. Remove steak to a cutting board to rest.

5 Carefully place hot skillet over medium-high heat on the stovetop and add seasoned shrimp. Cook shrimp 4 minutes, flipping one time halfway through cooking. Transfer shrimp to four dinner plates and return skillet to stovetop over medium heat.

Continued ▶

6 Add snap peas and butter to skillet and cook 3 minutes, stirring frequently. Divide snap peas onto dinner plates with shrimp.

7 Slice steak against the grain into $\frac{1}{4}$"-thick slices, then divide among dinner plates and serve immediately.

PER SERVING
Calories: 299 | Fat: 13g | Protein: 36g | Sodium: 52mg | Fiber: 3g | Carbohydrates: 9g | Sugar: 5g

Tips, Substitutions, and More...

Cooking times for steak are based on 1" steak thickness and will need to be adjusted for thinner or thicker steaks. Boneless rib eye can be swapped for the strip steak. The instructions are for medium-rare doneness or 145°F after resting time.

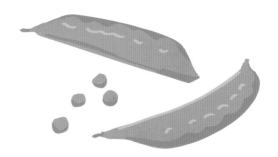

Lemon Dijon Chicken with Orzo and Peas

SERVES
4

Orzo is a quick-cooking small grain pasta with a shape slightly larger than rice. By cooking the orzo directly in the skillet, you are able to utilize the natural starch that is released by the orzo during the cooking process to help create a creamy and thick sauce. Add lemon, Dijon mustard, chicken, and peas and you have a wonderful one pot dinner that satisfies everyone!

PREP TIME: 8 MINUTES • ACTIVE COOK TIME: 20 MINUTES • HANDS-OFF COOK TIME: N/A

$1^1/2$ teaspoons kosher salt

2 teaspoons dried parsley

$^1/2$ teaspoon ground black pepper

$^1/2$ teaspoon paprika

$^1/2$ teaspoon dried thyme

2 tablespoons extra-virgin olive oil

$1^1/2$ pounds boneless, skinless chicken thighs, cut into 1" chunks

$1^1/2$ cups uncooked orzo pasta

3 cups low-sodium chicken broth

1 cup frozen peas

4 cloves garlic, peeled and crushed

$^1/2$ cup half-and-half

2 tablespoons Dijon mustard

Zest and juice of 1 medium lemon

1. In a small dish, combine salt, parsley, pepper, paprika, and thyme; set aside.

2. Heat a 12" or larger cast iron skillet over medium-high heat. Once hot, add oil and chicken. Sprinkle half of spice mixture over chicken and cook 2 minutes.

3. Flip chicken pieces and sprinkle remaining spice mixture over the other side. Cook an additional 2 minutes.

4. Add orzo and broth to skillet, stir to combine, and bring to a boil.

5. Once boiling, immediately reduce heat to medium. Continue simmering 12 minutes, stirring frequently.

6. Add peas and garlic to skillet. Stir to mix and continue cooking an additional 1 minute. Slowly add half-and-half and mustard, continuously stirring until well incorporated, about 1 minute.

7. Add lemon zest and juice and stir until completely mixed, about 1 minute. Serve.

PER SERVING
Calories: 528 | Fat: 26g | Protein: 44g | Sodium: 1,010mg | Fiber: 2g | Carbohydrates: 29g | Sugar: 7g

Loaded Three-Cheese and Refried Bean Skillet Nachos

SERVES
4

The secret to creating restaurant-worthy nachos at home is using thick-cut tortilla chips and taking the time to layer the chips and cheese before the skillet goes into the oven. If you have leftover cooked chicken, beef, or pork on hand, add it along with the refried beans for even more protein and flavor. If you have leftover guacamole, add $\frac{1}{2}$ cup to this recipe in place of the avocados.

PREP TIME: 10 MINUTES ● ACTIVE COOK TIME: N/A ● HANDS-OFF COOK TIME: 15 MINUTES

12 ounces thick-cut tortilla chips

16 ounces shredded Mexican cheese blend

2 (15-ounce) cans refried beans

$\frac{1}{2}$ cup full-fat sour cream

$1\frac{1}{2}$ tablespoons whole milk

12 ounces mild pico de gallo

$\frac{1}{4}$ cup pickled, sliced jalapeños, strained

2 medium scallions, thinly sliced

2 medium avocados, peeled, pitted, and diced

1 Preheat oven to 375°F. In a 12" or larger cast iron skillet, layer $\frac{1}{3}$ of chips, $\frac{1}{3}$ of cheese, and $\frac{1}{3}$ of refried beans. Repeat for a total of three layers.

2 Bake on center rack undisturbed 15 minutes or until cheese is melted and bubbly.

3 While nachos are baking, in a small bowl combine sour cream with $1\frac{1}{2}$ tablespoons milk to thin out so it is easy to drizzle. You may need an additional $\frac{1}{2}$ tablespoon milk to get a pourable consistency.

4 Remove skillet and top nachos with pico de gallo, sour cream drizzle, pickled jalapenos, sliced scallions, and avocado. Serve immediately.

Tips, Substitutions, and More...

For a spicy version, swap thinly sliced fresh jalapeños for the pickled jalapeños and hot pico de gallo for the mild.

PER SERVING
Calories: 939 | Fat: 50g | Protein: 32g | Sodium: 1,650mg | Fiber: 15g | Carbohydrates: 90g | Sugar: 8g

Chicken Thighs with Chickpeas and Feta

SERVES
4

This comforting one pan dinner is loaded with chickpeas, spinach, spices, and the perfect amount of warmed feta cheese over bone-in, crispy-skin chicken thighs. Start this dish on the stovetop and transfer to the oven, then sit back and let the oven work its magic while you decompress and wait for a delicious dinner!

PREP TIME: 4 MINUTES ● ACTIVE COOK TIME: 8 MINUTES ● HANDS-OFF COOK TIME: 30 MINUTES

4 large or 6 small (about 1^3/$_4$ pounds) skin-on, bone-in chicken thighs

2^1/$_2$ teaspoons smoked paprika, divided

2^1/$_2$ teaspoons Italian seasoning, divided

2 teaspoons kosher salt, divided

3 tablespoons extra-virgin olive oil

1 (5-ounce) bag fresh baby spinach

1 (14-ounce) can diced no-salt tomatoes, drained

1 (15-ounce) can chickpeas, drained with ^{1}/$_4$ cup liquid reserved

4 ounces Greek feta cheese, crumbled

1 Preheat oven to 400°F.

2 Place chicken on a cutting board or dinner plate and rub both sides with 2 teaspoons paprika, 2 teaspoons Italian seasoning, and 1 teaspoon salt.

3 Heat a 12" cast iron skillet over medium-high heat.

4 Once hot, add oil and chicken, skin side down. Cook undisturbed 5 minutes or until skin is crispy and browned. Wash dinner plate or cutting board during cooking, then transfer partially cooked chicken back to the dinner plate or cutting board (keep skin side up) and set aside.

5 Add spinach, tomatoes, chickpeas with ^{1}/$_4$ cup chickpea liquid, and remaining spices to skillet. Sauté 3 minutes, stirring frequently, or until spinach is completely wilted and spices are well mixed.

Continued ▶

6 Turn off heat. Nestle chicken thighs (skin side up) into spinach mixture. Sprinkle feta over spinach mixture, taking care to avoid placing feta directly onto crispy chicken skin.

7 Bake on center rack uncovered 30 minutes or until chicken thighs reach 165°F internal temperature. Allow the skillet to rest 5 minutes before serving.

PER SERVING
Calories: 591 | Fat: 22g | Protein: 20g | Sodium: 1,365mg | Fiber: 12g | Carbohydrates: 77g | Sugar: 19g

Tips, Substitutions, and More...

For a kick of heat, add $\frac{1}{2}$ teaspoon crushed red pepper flakes to the spinach mixture along with the tomatoes. Optional toppings for this dish are freshly chopped basil, cilantro, or parsley.

Shredded Chicken Chilaquiles Verde

SERVES 4

This simplified version of chilaquiles uses high-quality store-bought salsa verde, already shredded rotisserie chicken, and thick-cut tortilla chips. Top with crumbled cotija cheese, fresh cilantro, and a sour cream drizzle for a delicious and fast dinner. Serve with your favorite hot sauce for a kick of heat!

PREP TIME: 10 MINUTES • ACTIVE COOK TIME: 5 MINUTES • HANDS-OFF COOK TIME: N/A

1 tablespoon avocado oil

24 ounces salsa verde

12 ounces shredded rotisserie chicken

6 ounces thick-cut tortilla chips

2.5 ounces cotija cheese, crumbled

1/4 cup chopped fresh cilantro leaves

1/2 cup full-fat sour cream

2 tablespoons whole milk

1. Heat a 12" or larger cast iron skillet over medium heat. Once hot, add oil, salsa, and chicken. Stir occasionally, until warmed through, 3 minutes.

2. Gently add tortilla chips to skillet and carefully fold them into salsa, taking care not to break them, until covered with sauce, about 2 minutes. Transfer to a serving plate and top with cheese and cilantro.

3. In a measuring cup or small bowl, combine sour cream with milk, then drizzle over chilaquiles. Serve immediately.

PER SERVING
Calories: 558 | Fat: 36g | Protein: 26g | Sodium: 1,269mg | Fiber: 4g | Carbohydrates: 33g | Sugar: 9g

Tips, Substitutions, and More...

Since every brand of salsa has variable salt levels, you may need to add a bit more salt to the sauce. Taste and add in 1/4 teaspoon increments. No rotisserie chicken on hand? Scramble 2–3 eggs per person and add after you plate the chilaquiles before you crumble on the cheese. Additional topping options are: thinly sliced sweet onions or scallions, refried beans, and cubed avocado or guacamole.

Pierogi, Andouille Sausage, and Onion Skillet

This simple but flavor-packed dinner is made in around 20 minutes with a handful of easy-to-find ingredients, including frozen pierogies. No need for another pot to precook the pierogies. Chorizo or hot Italian sausage can be swapped for the andouille sausage.

PREP TIME: 5 MINUTES ● ACTIVE COOK TIME: 16 MINUTES ● HANDS-OFF COOK TIME: N/A

2 tablespoons extra-virgin olive oil

1 pound uncooked andouille sausage, crumbled

1 medium yellow onion, peeled, halved, and thinly sliced

8 ounces grape tomatoes

1 pound frozen potato and cheese pierogi

1/2 cup heavy cream

1 Heat a 12" or larger cast iron skillet over medium-high heat. Once hot, add oil, sausage, onion, and tomatoes. Sauté 5 minutes, stirring occasionally, or until sausage begins to brown.

2 Use spatula to burst tomatoes by pressing down on each one so the juices release.

3 Add pierogies to skillet and stir to combine. Cover with lid and lower heat to medium. Cook 6–8 minutes until pierogies are soft and warm in the center.

4 Remove lid, add heavy cream, and stir to combine. Simmer 2–3 minutes, stirring, until sauce thickens. Remove from heat and serve immediately.

PER SERVING
Calories: 1,185 | Fat: 52g | Protein: 43g |
Sodium: 1,618mg | Fiber: 7g | Carbohydrates: 137g |
Sugar: 5g

Tips, Substitutions, and More...

Every brand of andouille sausage has a different saltiness, so you can add additional salt (if needed) in 1/4 teaspoon increments at the end of cooking. To substitute fresh or refrigerated pierogies, add to the pan at the same point in the recipe and cover but reduce the cooking time to 2–3 minutes.

Italian Sausage and White Bean Skillet with Tortellini

SERVES 4

Quick-cooking cheese tortellini are combined with Italian sausage, spices, and a handful of other delicious ingredients for a complete skillet dinner that is loaded with flavor and free from laborious prep work.

PREP TIME: 5 MINUTES • ACTIVE COOK TIME: 12 MINUTES • HANDS-OFF COOK TIME: N/A

2 tablespoons extra-virgin olive oil

1 pound bulk uncooked mild Italian sausage, crumbled

1 (5-ounce) bag fresh baby spinach

1 cup low-sodium chicken broth

3/4 teaspoon kosher salt

1/2 teaspoon Italian seasoning

1/4 teaspoon ground black pepper

2 cloves garlic, peeled and crushed

1 (15-ounce) can white beans, drained and rinsed

1 1/2 pounds uncooked refrigerated cheese tortellini

1/4 cup heavy cream

1/2 cup grated Parmesan cheese

1 Heat a 12" or larger cast iron skillet over medium-high heat. Once hot, add oil and sausage, and cook undisturbed 3 minutes.

2 Use a spatula to break up sausage and flip, cooking an additional 3 minutes or until most of the pink is gone. Add spinach, stir to combine, and cook 1 minute or until wilted.

3 Add broth, spices, garlic, beans, and tortellini to skillet; stir to combine and bring to a boil. Once boiling, immediately lower heat to medium, add heavy cream, and stir to combine. Simmer, stirring frequently, 2 minutes or until sauce thickens.

4 Remove from heat, stir in Parmesan, and serve.

PER SERVING
Calories: 980 | Fat: 46g | Protein: 44g | Sodium: 1,702mg | Fiber: 9g | Carbohydrates: 82g | Sugar: 7g

Tips, Substitutions, and More...

Shredded Parmesan cheese can be substituted for grated Parmesan cheese. Swap in hot Italian sausage to add some heat. While this recipe calls for cheese tortellini, feel free to swap in your favorite savory tortellini. For frozen tortellini, add tortellini as called for in recipe, cover with lid, and add an additional 4 minutes of cooking time after they come to a boil. Remove the lid and continue with directions.

Quick Beef Enchilada Skillet

SERVES 5

Use your skillet to create this flavor-packed Quick Beef Enchilada Skillet in no time. Loaded with ground beef, beans, corn, spices, enchilada sauce, and tortillas, this recipe makes an amazing dinner as-is or with your favorite toppings!

PREP TIME: 8 MINUTES • ACTIVE COOK TIME: 7 MINUTES • HANDS-OFF COOK TIME: 12 MINUTES

2 tablespoons avocado oil

1 medium yellow onion, peeled, quartered, and thinly sliced

1 1/2 pounds 80% lean ground beef

2 teaspoons chili powder

1 teaspoon kosher salt

1 teaspoon ground cumin

1 teaspoon dried oregano

1 (15-ounce) can pinto beans, drained and rinsed

1 (4-ounce) can diced green chiles

1/2 cup frozen sweet corn kernels

1 (15-ounce) jar enchilada sauce

6 (6") corn tortillas, cut into 1/2" strips

2 cups shredded Mexican cheese blend

1/2 cup full-fat sour cream

1 (8-ounce) bag shredded iceberg lettuce

1/4 cup fresh cilantro leaves

1 Preheat oven to 425°F.

2 Heat a 12" or larger cast iron skillet over medium-high heat. Once hot, add oil, onion, ground beef, and spices. Sauté 5 minutes, stirring occasionally, or until beef is mostly cooked through and onions begin to soften.

3 Stir in beans, chiles, corn, and enchilada sauce. Cook 2 minutes to warm through. Turn off heat.

4 Add tortilla strips to skillet and stir until covered with sauce. Top with cheese. Bake uncovered on center rack 12 minutes or until the cheese is completely melted.

5 Serve topped with sour cream, lettuce, and cilantro leaves.

PER SERVING
Calories: 798 | Fat: 51g | Protein: 42g | Sodium: 1,358mg | Fiber: 11g | Carbohydrates: 42g | Sugar: 6g

Tips, Substitutions, and More...

Swap in shredded Cheddar cheese if preferred. Canned kidney or black beans can be substituted for pinto beans. For a bit of heat, use spicy enchilada sauce. Additional topping ideas include sliced scallions, diced avocado or guacamole, pickled jalapeños, pico de gallo, and your favorite hot sauce.

CHAPTER THREE
DUTCH OVEN DINNERS

51

Meet the Dutch oven aka the one pot wonder! One of the unique elements of the Dutch oven is that it is both stovetop and oven safe, meaning you can start a dish on the stovetop for browning, sautéing, or simmering and then transfer to the oven to finish cooking with hands-off cook time.

In this chapter, you will find an array of one pot Dutch oven dinner recipes that span the culinary spectrum. From a Roman-style 5-Ingredient Authentic Fettuccine Alfredo ready in under 15 minutes, to a ridiculously delicious White Bean and Spinach Chicken Bake with Panko Parmesan topping, to cozy comforts like Turkey Potpie with Biscuit Crust, the Dutch oven will quickly become a dependable and trustworthy kitchen tool for your one pot dinners.

5-Ingredient Authentic Fettuccine Alfredo

SERVES
4

Authentic Roman fettuccine Alfredo isn't made with heavy cream or flour and is traditionally made with only pasta, pasta cooking water, butter, and Parmesan cheese. The secret is cooking the pasta in a small amount of water so that the water is super starchy. Then, use that starchy water to create a sauce in 1 minute with melted butter and very finely grated Parmesan cheese. This easy version adds some black pepper for a bite.

PREP TIME: 2 MINUTES ● ACTIVE COOK TIME: 12 MINUTES ● HANDS-OFF COOK TIME: N/A

2 tablespoons plus $1/4$ teaspoon kosher salt, divided

1 pound uncooked fettuccine pasta

1 cup reserved pasta cooking liquid

1 stick ($1/2$ cup) unsalted butter, cubed

$1/2$ teaspoon freshly ground black pepper

4 ounces plus 4 teaspoons finely grated Parmesan cheese, divided

1 Fill a 5.5-quart or larger Dutch oven halfway with cold water and add 2 tablespoons salt. Bring to a boil over high heat.

2 Cook fettuccine according to package directions minus 1 minute (you will finish cooking it in the sauce), stirring occasionally, about 7–9 minutes. Once pasta is al dente (almost cooked), use a glass measuring cup or mug to reserve 1 cup of pasta cooking water and set aside.

3 Strain pasta into a colander and return Dutch oven back to stovetop over medium heat.

4 Add in $1/2$ cup pasta cooking water, butter, pepper, and remaining $1/4$ teaspoon salt. Whisk to dissolve butter, 30–45 seconds.

5 Begin whisking in 4 ounces Parmesan and continue until cheese is dissolved and a creamy sauce forms, approximately 1 minute.

Continued ▶

6 Keep Dutch oven on the stovetop but turn off heat. Add strained pasta and toss until pasta is well coated with sauce, about 1 minute. Add additional pasta cooking water if needed (in 1 tablespoon increments).

7 Serve immediately topped with remaining 4 teaspoons Parmesan.

PER SERVING
Calories: 644 | Fat: 28g | Protein: 20g | Sodium: 1,255mg | Fiber: 4g | Carbohydrates: 20g | Sugar: 0g

Tips, Substitutions, and More...

The quality of Parmesan cheese really matters for this simple dish. Look for a young Parmesan like a twelve-month Parmigiano-Reggiano as it will be sweeter. The longer Parmesan ages, the more bite it gets and it can taste bitter in a dish like this. To make this sauce this quickly, the Parmesan must be finely grated. Linguine can be substituted for fettuccine if preferred. Don't have unsalted butter? Omit the 1/4 teaspoon kosher salt from the sauce and use salted butter. For a kick of heat, serve with crushed red pepper flakes. To add more protein, toss in leftover chicken or cooked shrimp with the pasta.

Adobo-Rubbed Lamb Loin Chops with Kale and Couscous

SERVES 4

Use your Dutch oven to perfectly cook seasoned lamb loin chops and finish cooking your side dishes in the amount of time needed for the lamb to rest using the same pot! Maximum flavor, minimal cleanup, and a complete dinner in just 25 minutes.

PREP TIME: 5 MINUTES ● ACTIVE COOK TIME: 9 MINUTES ● HANDS-OFF COOK TIME: 11 MINUTES

4 (6-ounce) lamb loin chops

3 tablespoons adobo seasoning, divided

2 tablespoons extra-virgin olive oil

2 tablespoons salted butter

6 ounces cleaned and chopped fresh kale

1½ cups low-sodium chicken broth

3 cloves garlic, peeled and crushed

1½ cups uncooked couscous

1 medium lemon, quartered

1. Bring lamb chops out of refrigerator about 30 minutes before cooking. While resting on the counter, rub 2 tablespoons adobo seasoning on all sides of chops.

2. Heat a 5.5-quart or larger Dutch oven over medium-high heat. Once hot, add oil and then lamb chops. Cook undisturbed 3 minutes. Flip and cook an additional 3 minutes on the other side.

3. Reduce heat to medium, cover, and cook 6 minutes. Remove lamb chops to a cutting board. Set aside.

4. Return Dutch oven to stovetop and set over medium-high heat. Add butter and kale. Sauté, stirring constantly, 2 minutes or until kale is wilted. Add broth, garlic, and remaining 1 tablespoon adobo seasoning and stir to combine.

5. As soon as broth begins to bubble, turn off heat and add couscous. Working quickly, stir to combine and use a spoon or spatula to make sure all couscous is submerged under broth. Cover and let sit 5 minutes.

6. Remove lid, fluff couscous, and serve alongside lamb chops with lemon wedge. Squeeze lemon over lamb and couscous.

PER SERVING
Calories: 400 | Fat: 25g | Protein: 39g | Sodium: 2,417mg |
Fiber: 1g | Carbohydrates: 5g | Sugar: 0g

Shortcut Shakshuka with Feta

While the authentic version of this popular Mediterranean meal starts with a sofrito and uses fresh chopped tomatoes, this shortcut version saves all of the chopping time by harnessing the power of high-quality store-bought marinara sauce, crushed garlic, and a select group of spices. Topped with crumbled feta cheese and served with crusty bread, this vegetarian meal is a keeper!

PREP TIME: 2 MINUTES ● ACTIVE COOK TIME: 2 MINUTES ● HANDS-OFF COOK TIME: 8 MINUTES

¼ cup extra-virgin olive oil

1 (24-ounce) jar marinara sauce

1 teaspoon ground cumin

1 teaspoon smoked paprika

½ teaspoon crushed red pepper flakes

¼ teaspoon kosher salt

¼ teaspoon ground black pepper

4 cloves garlic, peeled and crushed

1 (5-ounce) bag fresh baby spinach

8 large eggs

4 ounces Greek feta cheese, crumbled

1 (12-ounce) loaf crusty white bread, cut into 8 slices

1   Heat a 5.5-quart or larger Dutch oven over medium heat. Once hot, add oil, sauce, spices, garlic, and spinach. Stir to combine and cook 2 minutes or until spinach begins to wilt.

2   Use a wooden spoon to make eight spaced-out wells or indentions in the mixture. Gently crack an egg into each well so that they settle into sauce to cook. Cover and simmer 8 minutes for egg whites to set. If you don't like runny yolks, add an additional 2–4 minutes for yolks to set.

3   Top with feta. Serve immediately with crusty bread.

PER SERVING
Calories: 683 | Fat: 34g | Protein: 29g | Sodium: 1,350mg | Fiber: 6g | Carbohydrates: 65g | Sugar: 12g

Salmon with Toasted Garlic, Tomatoes, and Pearl Couscous

SERVES 4

Quickly create a blast of flavor by toasting sliced garlic and combining it with spices before adding pearl couscous, olives, and canned tomatoes. Nestle in wild Alaskan salmon fillets, place the lid on, and about 15 minutes later, you have a wonderful dinner with only one pot to wash.

PREP TIME: 5 MINUTES ● ACTIVE COOK TIME: 3 MINUTES ● HANDS-OFF COOK TIME: 17 MINUTES

3 tablespoons extra-virgin olive oil

6 cloves garlic, peeled and thinly sliced

1$\frac{1}{2}$ teaspoons kosher salt

$\frac{1}{2}$ teaspoon ground cumin

$\frac{1}{2}$ teaspoon smoked paprika

$\frac{1}{4}$ teaspoon ground black pepper

$\frac{1}{4}$ teaspoon turmeric

$\frac{1}{4}$ teaspoon dried thyme

4 ounces cleaned and chopped fresh kale

1$\frac{1}{2}$ cups uncooked pearl couscous

1$\frac{3}{4}$ cups low-sodium chicken broth

1 (14.5-ounce) can diced no-salt tomatoes

24 pitted kalamata olives

1$\frac{1}{2}$ pounds wild Alaskan salmon fillets

1 Heat a 5.5-quart or larger Dutch oven over medium-high heat. Once hot, add oil, garlic, and spices. Sauté 30 seconds, stirring constantly. Add kale and couscous, and continue cooking 1 minute, stirring frequently to help wilt kale.

2 Add broth, tomatoes, and olives, and bring to a boil still over medium-high heat. Once boiling, gently nestle salmon on top, pushing down slightly but taking care to keep couscous under broth mixture. Reduce heat to medium, cover, and cook undisturbed 14 minutes.

3 Remove from heat, do not open lid, and allow the Dutch oven to rest with lid on for 3 minutes before serving.

PER SERVING
Calories: 685 | Fat: 39g | Protein: 24g | Sodium: 920mg | Fiber: 37g | Carbohydrates: 56g | Sugar: 8g

Tips, Substitutions, and More…

Save additional time by skipping sliced garlic. Just increase the garlic cloves to 8 and crush with garlic press. Baby spinach can be substituted for kale. Some additional topping options when serving are crumbled feta cheese over the couscous and freshly chopped parsley.

White Bean and Spinach Chicken Bake with Panko Parmesan

SERVES 6

This White Bean and Spinach Chicken Bake is loaded with chunks of chicken, white beans, spinach, pasta shells, and a creamy delicious Boursin cheese sauce. Start on the stovetop and in just 8 minutes, transfer to the oven for mostly hands-off cooking. Then 10 minutes before cooking time is up, add the panko and Parmesan crust and bake until it's brown and crispy!

PREP TIME: 10 MINUTES • ACTIVE COOK TIME: 8 MINUTES • HANDS-OFF COOK TIME: 40 MINUTES

For Topping

1 cup panko bread crumbs

1/4 cup grated Parmesan cheese

1 teaspoon dried parsley

1/2 teaspoon smoked paprika

1/4 teaspoon kosher salt

2 tablespoons extra-virgin olive oil

1 To make Topping: Combine ingredients in a small bowl. Set aside.

For Chicken Bake

2 tablespoons salted butter

1 medium yellow onion, peeled, quartered, and thinly sliced

2 medium stalks celery, diced

1 1/4 teaspoons kosher salt

1/2 teaspoon ground black pepper

1/2 teaspoon cayenne pepper

1 pound boneless, skinless chicken breast, cut into 1" chunks

2 To make Chicken Bake: Preheat oven to 400°F.

3 Heat a 5.5-quart or larger Dutch oven on the stovetop over medium-high heat. Once hot, add butter, onion, celery, and spices. Sauté 2 minutes, stirring frequently.

4 Add chicken and spinach, cook 3 minutes, stirring occasionally, or until spinach is completely wilted and some pieces of chicken are beginning to brown.

1 (5-ounce) bag fresh
baby spinach

2 cups low-sodium chicken broth

2 (5.2-ounce) packages Boursin
Garlic & Fine Herbs cheese

1 (15-ounce) can white beans,
drained and rinsed

8 ounces small uncooked
pasta shells

5 Stir in broth. Crumble Boursin cheese into broth mixture and stir until completely dissolved, about 1 minute; bring to a boil.

6 As soon as the mixture is bubbling, turn off heat and add beans and pasta. Use a spatula or spoon to push pasta under liquid. Place the lid on the Dutch oven and bake on center rack of oven 30 minutes.

7 Remove Dutch oven to a heat-safe surface. Remove lid and stir to mix pasta shells. Scrape down the sides so that all of the ingredients are under remaining sauce.

8 Top pasta mixture with prepared Topping. Return to oven and bake uncovered 10 minutes. Remove and allow to rest uncovered 5 minutes before serving.

PER SERVING
Calories: 658 | Fat: 34g | Protein: 34g | Sodium: 931mg | Fiber: 6g | Carbohydrates: 54g | Sugar: 4g

Tips, Substitutions, and More...

Don't have shells? Another small, sturdy pasta shape can be swapped in such as fusilli, orecchiette, penne, or even macaroni. Save even more time by using a package of ground chicken breast to skip prepping the chicken breast. It's recommended to crumble into larger chunks for texture.

Turkey Potpie with Biscuit Crust

Traditional potpie recipes can be quite the labor of love. This shortcut version saves almost all of the labor by using leftover turkey (or chicken), frozen mixed vegetables, and refrigerated biscuit dough to create a potpie in no time.

PREP TIME: 5 MINUTES ● ACTIVE COOK TIME: 9 MINUTES ● HANDS-OFF COOK TIME: 25 MINUTES

4 tablespoons salted butter

1 medium yellow onion, peeled and chopped

1 pound frozen mixed vegetables (peas, carrots, corn, green beans)

1/4 cup all-purpose flour

1 1/4 teaspoons kosher salt

1/2 teaspoon ground black pepper

1/2 teaspoon dried thyme

2 cups low-sodium chicken broth

2/3 cup heavy cream

1 pound leftover cubed or shredded turkey meat

1 (16-ounce) package refrigerated flaky biscuits

Tips, Substitutions, and More...

Substitute cubed or shredded rotisserie chicken or leftover chicken for turkey. When arranging the biscuit dough, leave a little space between biscuits or around the edge of the potpie as the sauce will bubble up when cooking.

1 Preheat oven to 350°F.

2 Heat a 5.5-quart or larger Dutch oven on the stovetop over medium-high heat. Once hot, add butter and stir until melted. Then add onion and frozen vegetables. Sauté 5 minutes, stirring frequently.

3 Stir in flour and spices, reduce heat to medium, and cook 2 minutes, stirring continuously, or until flour begins to brown.

4 Add broth and heavy cream. Continue cooking, stirring occasionally, 1–2 minutes, until sauce begins to bubble.

5 Immediately remove from heat, then stir in turkey. Arrange biscuit dough on top of turkey mixture so that biscuits are evenly covering top of potpie.

6 Bake uncovered on center rack 25 minutes or until the sauce is bubbling and biscuits are light brown on top. Allow to cool 10 minutes and serve.

PER SERVING
Calories: 611 | Fat: 34g | Protein: 31g | Sodium: 1,193mg | Fiber: 4g | Carbohydrates: 45g | Sugar: 9g

Hungarian Chicken Paprikash over Egg Noodles

SERVES 4

This shortcut version of chicken paprikash saves cooking time by swapping boneless, skinless chicken thighs for the traditional bone-in thighs and by using the same pot for cooking both the noodles and the chicken to minimize cleanup. A delicious comfort food dinner done in just 40 minutes!

PREP TIME: 10 MINUTES • ACTIVE COOK TIME: 18 MINUTES • HANDS-OFF COOK TIME: 12 MINUTES

2 tablespoons plus 2$\frac{1}{2}$ teaspoons kosher salt, divided

8 ounces uncooked wide egg noodles

4 tablespoons salted butter, divided

4 large or 6 small (about 2 pounds total) boneless, skinless chicken thighs

$\frac{3}{4}$ teaspoon ground black pepper, divided

1 large yellow onion, peeled, halved, and thinly sliced

4 cloves garlic, peeled and crushed

2 tablespoons all-purpose flour

2 tablespoons tomato paste

3$\frac{1}{2}$ tablespoons Hungarian sweet paprika

2 cups low-sodium chicken broth

$\frac{3}{4}$ cup full-fat sour cream

$\frac{1}{2}$ cup finely chopped fresh flat-leaf parsley

1 Fill a 5.5-quart or larger Dutch oven halfway with water. Add 2 tablespoons salt. Bring to a boil over high heat.

2 Cook egg noodles according to package instructions (6–8 minutes depending on thickness and brand), minus 1 minute. Drain and reserve drained egg noodles in a mixing bowl covered with plastic wrap to keep them warm.

3 Return Dutch oven to stovetop over medium-high heat. Once hot, add 2 tablespoons butter and chicken thighs. Sprinkle thighs with $\frac{1}{4}$ teaspoon each of salt and pepper. Cook undisturbed 3 minutes.

4 Flip thighs, sprinkle other side with $\frac{1}{4}$ teaspoon each of salt and pepper, and cook undisturbed another 3 minutes. Remove thighs to a dinner plate and set aside.

5 Add remaining 2 tablespoons butter, onion, and remaining 2 teaspoons salt and $1/4$ teaspoon pepper to the Dutch oven. Sauté 4 minutes, stirring frequently, or until onions begin to soften. Add garlic, flour, tomato paste, and paprika, stir to combine, and sauté 30–45 seconds until garlic is fragrant.

6 Pour in broth and whisk until mixed well. Return partially cooked chicken thighs, cover, reduce heat to medium, and cook 12 minutes or until chicken is cooked through and reaches internal temperature of 165°F.

7 Turn off heat. Remove chicken thighs to a cutting board and use a chefs knife to quickly cut (on short side) into $1/2$" strips.

8 While the chicken is resting on the cutting board, slowly whisk sour cream into the sauce in small spoonfuls (so it doesn't curdle).

9 Return chicken pieces to sauce and stir to coat. Divide warm egg noodles onto four plates, top with chicken and sauce, and serve immediately, topped with parsley.

PER SERVING
Calories: 788 | Fat: 42g | Protein: 51g | Sodium: 917mg | Fiber: 3g | Carbohydrates: 51g | Sugar: 6g

No-Mix Cheesy Meatball Subs

SERVES 5

Making traditional meatballs is a time-consuming process. This recipe utilizes the hack of rolling bulk Italian sausage into meatballs to bypass the prep work of having to season the meat, which usually includes chopping, measuring, and more. Use mild or hot Italian sausage depending on your spice preference.

PREP TIME: 8 MINUTES • ACTIVE COOK TIME: 10 MINUTES • HANDS-OFF COOK TIME: 30 MINUTES

2 pounds bulk uncooked Italian sausage

2 tablespoons extra-virgin olive oil

1 (24-ounce) jar marinara sauce

5 (6") white hoagie rolls

5 (1-ounce) slices provolone cheese

5 teaspoons grated Parmesan cheese

1/4 cup thinly sliced fresh basil

1 Divide sausage into 16 sections. Roll each section into a meatball and set aside.

2 Place a 5.5-quart or larger Dutch oven over medium-high heat. Once hot, add oil and then meatballs in a single layer. It's okay if they touch slightly. Cook undisturbed 5 minutes. Gently flip meatballs and cook on opposite side an additional 5 minutes.

3 Reduce heat to medium-low, add marinara sauce, and cover. Simmer meatballs 30 minutes, stirring occasionally. Remove lid and allow meatballs and sauce to rest 10 minutes.

4 To serve, line each roll with a slice of provolone, place three meatballs on each roll, and top each with 1 teaspoon Parmesan. Sprinkle with sliced basil.

Tips, Substitutions, and More...

You will have one leftover meatball—it makes a great snack! Depending on the shape of your Dutch oven, you may need to sauté meatballs in batches. Don't skip the provolone cheese: Lining the roll with the cheese helps protect the bread from getting soggy. If you have a few extra minutes, toasting the bread is highly recommended.

PER SERVING
Calories: 846 | Fat: 54g | Protein: 43g | Sodium: 2,201mg | Fiber: 3g | Carbohydrates: 47g | Sugar: 10g

Creamy Pesto Pasta with Salami

This one pot pasta dinner uses the hack of cooking the pasta directly in the sauce to avoid the hassle of having to boil the pasta separately and then strain it. This eliminates prep and cleanup time and delivers a full meal in under 30 minutes!

PREP TIME: 3 MINUTES • ACTIVE COOK TIME: 20 MINUTES • HANDS-OFF COOK TIME: 1 MINUTE

2 tablespoons extra-virgin olive oil

8 ounces Genoa salami, diced

4 cups low-sodium chicken broth

1 (8-ounce) package full-fat cream cheese, cut into 8 cubes

1 cup basil pesto

1/2 teaspoon kosher salt

1/4 teaspoon ground black pepper

1 pound uncooked fusilli pasta

1 (5-ounce) bag fresh baby spinach

1/2 cup grated Parmesan cheese

1 Heat a 5.5-quart or larger Dutch oven over medium-high heat. Once hot, add oil and salami. Cook 3 minutes, stirring occasionally.

2 Add broth, cream cheese, pesto, salt, and pepper; whisk to dissolve cream cheese. Once dissolved, increase heat to high and bring mixture to a boil.

3 Once boiling, add pasta and reduce heat to medium. Cook 12–15 minutes, stirring frequently until most excess liquid is absorbed and you are left with a thick and creamy sauce, and pasta is tender but not overcooked.

4 Remove from heat and stir in spinach and Parmesan. Cover 1 minute for spinach to wilt. Serve.

PER SERVING
Calories: 617 | Fat: 42g | Protein: 26g | Sodium: 1,426mg | Fiber: 24g | Carbohydrates: 34g | Sugar: 3g

Dutch Oven Beef and Bean Tamale Pie

SERVES
6

Start this chili "pie" on the stovetop. Less than 10 minutes later, pop it into the oven to finish cooking completely hands-off. This hearty meal uses crumbled prepared polenta as a hack to mimic corn bread topping without any of the extra work.

PREP TIME: 10 MINUTES • ACTIVE COOK TIME: 7 MINUTES • HANDS-OFF COOK TIME: 30 MINUTES

2 tablespoons avocado oil

1 large yellow onion, peeled and chopped

2 large stalks celery, chopped

6 cloves garlic, peeled and crushed

1½ pounds 80% lean ground beef

4 tablespoons chili powder

1 tablespoon plus 1 teaspoon kosher salt

2 teaspoons ground cumin

1 teaspoon dried oregano

1 (28-ounce) can crushed tomatoes

1 (16-ounce) can tomato sauce

1 (4-ounce) can fire-roasted whole green chiles

2 (15-ounce) cans kidney beans, drained and rinsed

1 (18-ounce) tube prepared polenta, crumbled

8 ounces shredded Mexican cheese blend

1 Preheat oven to 375°F.

2 Heat a 5.5-quart or larger Dutch oven on the stovetop over medium-high heat. Once hot, add oil, followed by onion, celery, and garlic. Cook 3 minutes, stirring frequently.

3 Add ground beef and spices, and continue cooking 3 more minutes, stirring to break up beef into chunks. Add crushed tomatoes, tomato sauce, chiles, and beans. Stir to combine.

4 Remove from heat, add crumbled polenta (do not stir), and top with cheese. Bake uncovered on center rack 30 minutes.

5 Allow to cool 5 minutes before serving.

PER SERVING
Calories: 900 | Fat: 40g | Protein: 51g | Sodium: 2,092mg | Fiber: 24g | Carbohydrates: 84g | Sugar: 12g

CHAPTER FOUR

DINNERS IN A MIXING BOWL

Enjoy one pot dinners without *any* cooking time—either active or hands-off! All of the recipes in this chapter are created in only a mixing bowl along with the use of a cutting board. Most of the recipes take just 10 minutes or less of active prep time, and you won't find any sneaky instructions to bake, broil, grill, roast, or simmer anything before adding it to the mixing bowl.

Here you will find approachable recipes with prep work shortcuts, like Chopped Italian Sub Bowl and Greek-Inspired Chickpea Salad with Pita Bread, in addition to a flavor-packed focaccia sandwich made on a cutting board, where you use the mixing bowl to whip up a 1-minute Garlicky Creole Mayo that takes the sandwich to the next level. Have leftovers? Just cover the mixing bowl with plastic wrap and place it in the refrigerator; no need for any additional containers.

Panzanella Salad with Tuna and Fresh Mozzarella

SERVES
6

Inspired by the classic Italian salad from Tuscany, this protein-packed version utilizes the convenience of high-quality canned tuna to add quick protein without any additional prep or cook time. A simple, fresh, and satisfying dinner salad that won't leave you hungry.

PREP TIME: 15 MINUTES • ACTIVE COOK TIME: N/A • HANDS-OFF COOK TIME: N/A

1/2 cup extra-virgin olive oil

1/4 cup red wine vinegar

1 teaspoon kosher salt

1/2 teaspoon ground black pepper

1 pound (about 4 cups) day-old crusty Italian bread, cut into medium chunks

1 pound (about 4 cups) plum tomatoes, cut into medium chunks

1 medium English cucumber, peeled and cut into medium chunks

1/2 small sweet onion, peeled, halved, and sliced

1 cup fresh basil leaves, roughly chopped

1 (5-ounce) can water-packed albacore tuna, drained

1 (8-ounce) container mini mozzarella balls, drained

1 Place oil, vinegar, salt, and pepper into a large mixing bowl. Use a whisk or fork to combine.

2 Add remaining ingredients and mix well. Allow to sit 5 minutes so that some of the dressing can soak into bread.

3 Divide onto six dinner plates, and serve.

PER SERVING
Calories: 502 | Fat: 27g | Protein: 23g | Sodium: 773mg | Fiber: 1g | Carbohydrates: 42g | Sugar: 4g

Tips, Substitutions, and More...

Don't have day-old bread? Cut a fresh loaf into 1" pieces and toss them onto a baking sheet. Bake 10 minutes at 300°F to dry the bread out a bit. You don't want it toasted, just dried out around the edges.

Greek-Inspired Chickpea Salad with Pita Bread

SERVES
4

Traditional Greek salads almost always have green bell peppers, but to save time on prep work, this version replaces them with protein- and fiber-rich chickpeas, which only need to be drained and rinsed before being added to the mixing bowl.

PREP TIME: 10 MINUTES • ACTIVE COOK TIME: N/A • HANDS-OFF COOK TIME: N/A

1/4 cup extra-virgin olive oil

2 tablespoons red wine vinegar

1 teaspoon dried oregano

1/2 teaspoon kosher salt

1/2 teaspoon ground black pepper

1 (15-ounce) can chickpeas, drained and rinsed

4 ounces Greek feta cheese, crumbled

24 pitted kalamata olives

1 medium English cucumber, quartered and sliced

4 plum tomatoes, quartered

1/2 small red onion, peeled and thinly sliced

4 pita breads

1 In a large mixing bowl, add oil, vinegar, and spices. Mix until well combined.

2 Add remaining ingredients except pita bread and toss until mixed.

3 Serve immediately alongside pita bread.

PER SERVING
Calories: 583 | Fat: 23g | Protein: 20g | Sodium: 828mg | Fiber: 12g | Carbohydrates: 74g | Sugar: 4g

Tips, Substitutions, and More...

For additional protein, add hard-cooked eggs, leftover shrimp or chicken, or canned fish. If you have an extra couple of minutes, consider warming the pita bread. For a kick of heat, add 1/2 teaspoon crushed red pepper flakes.

Speedy Pesto Salmon and White Bean Lettuce Wraps

SERVES 4

Truly a speedy recipe, this dish come together in just 5 minutes with no other work needed! Combine canned salmon with basil pesto, mayonnaise, and white beans for a protein-packed salad loaded with flavor. These serve as lettuce wraps but if you feel like something heartier, serve as a sandwich or with buttery crackers.

PREP TIME: 5 MINUTES ● ACTIVE COOK TIME: N/A ● HANDS-OFF COOK TIME: N/A

1 (14.5-ounce) can wild salmon, skinless and boneless, drained

1/3 cup mayonnaise

1/4 cup basil pesto

1 (15.5-ounce) can white beans, drained and rinsed

1 head romaine lettuce (approximately 8 large leaves)

1 In a large mixing bowl, combine salmon, mayonnaise, and pesto. Fold in beans.

2 Spoon mixture into lettuce leaves, wrap up leaves, and serve.

PER SERVING
Calories: 465 | Fat: 25g | Protein: 36g | Sodium: 327mg | Fiber: 9g | Carbohydrates: 24g | Sugar: 2g

Tips, Substitutions, and More...

Canned tuna can be substituted for salmon. You can also try this with pita bread as a sandwich, or atop thickly sliced cucumber rounds.

Peanut Sauce Chicken and Cabbage Bowls

SERVES 4

Quickly create a flavorful peanut sauce in the mixing bowl before adding in rotisserie chicken, shredded cabbage (or slaw mix), and sliced scallions. Toss and serve with hot chili oil for a kick. Excellent served warm alongside rice or served chilled right from the refrigerator. Prefer chunky peanut butter to creamy? Feel free to swap it in!

PREP TIME: 10 MINUTES • ACTIVE COOK TIME: N/A • HANDS-OFF COOK TIME: N/A

1/2 cup salted creamy peanut butter

2 tablespoons low-sodium soy sauce

2 tablespoons maple syrup

2 tablespoons toasted sesame oil

2 tablespoons lime juice

1 teaspoon sriracha

1/2 teaspoon kosher salt

1/4 teaspoon ground ginger

1 tablespoon water

12 ounces shredded rotisserie chicken

1 (12-ounce) bag shredded cabbage

6 medium scallions, sliced

1 In a large mixing bowl, whisk together peanut butter, soy sauce, maple syrup, sesame oil, lime juice, sriracha, salt, and ginger. Add water (adding more as needed to thin out). You want the dressing to be thick enough to drip off of a spoon.

2 Stir in chicken, cabbage, and scallions. Serve chilled or gently warmed in the microwave on high, 60–90 seconds.

PER SERVING
Calories: 477 | Fat: 33g | Protein: 23g | Sodium: 1,370mg | Fiber: 4g | Carbohydrates: 22g | Sugar: 12g

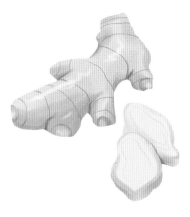

Rotisserie Chicken Caprese Salad

SERVES 4

A flavorful protein-packed meal ready in only 10 minutes! Serve with a baguette, inside a pita pocket, or as lettuce wraps for a low-carb option. For a heartier meal, pile atop warmed-up leftover rice or pasta.

PREP TIME: 10 MINUTES • ACTIVE COOK TIME: N/A • HANDS-OFF COOK TIME: N/A

6 tablespoons extra-virgin olive oil

3 tablespoons balsamic vinegar

1 1/2 teaspoons kosher salt

3/4 teaspoon ground black pepper

1 pound rotisserie chicken meat, shredded or cubed

1 pound grape tomatoes, halved top to bottom

1 (8-ounce) container mini mozzarella balls, drained

1 cup fresh basil leaves, thinly sliced

1 In a large mixing bowl, whisk oil, vinegar, salt, and pepper.

2 Add chicken, tomatoes, mozzarella, and basil. Toss until ingredients are well coated with dressing. Serve.

PER SERVING
Calories: 566 | Fat: 41g | Protein: 37g | Sodium: 800mg | Fiber: 2g | Carbohydrates: 11g | Sugar: 2g

Tips, Substitutions, and More...

Don't have mini mozzarella balls? Cube an 8-ounce ball of fresh mozzarella cheese. Substitute cherry tomatoes or quartered plum tomatoes for grape tomatoes. This dish can be served warm or chilled, whichever you prefer.

Focaccia with Smoked Turkey and Garlicky Creole Mayo

SERVES
4

For this 10-minute meal, put your mixing bowl to work to create a garlicky creole mayonnaise in under 1 minute. Spread on focaccia bread and combine with smoked turkey, Havarti cheese, tomato, onion, and arugula for a sandwich that will leave you drooling.

PREP TIME: 10 MINUTES • ACTIVE COOK TIME: N/A • HANDS-OFF COOK TIME: N/A

½ cup mayonnaise

1 clove garlic, peeled and crushed

1 tablespoon creole seasoning

1 (1-pound) loaf focaccia bread

12 ounces sliced smoked turkey breast

6 ounces sliced Havarti cheese

1 large beefsteak tomato, cut into 8 slices

½ small red onion, peeled and thinly sliced

½ cup baby arugula

1 In a small mixing bowl, combine mayonnaise, garlic, and creole seasoning. Set aside.

2 Use a serrated knife to slice focaccia loaf through center into a top and bottom. Place halves of focaccia on a cutting board with cut sides facing up.

3 Use a butter knife or spatula to spread creole mayonnaise evenly on cut sides of focaccia, using all of the mayonnaise. Layer turkey and cheese on bottom portion of focaccia.

4 Top with tomato, onion, and arugula. Place top portion of focaccia on top (cut side down) and cut into four sections. Serve immediately.

PER SERVING
Calories: 718 | Fat: 44g | Protein: 36g | Sodium: 1,206mg | Fiber: 3g | Carbohydrates: 45g | Sugar: 6g

Tips, Substitutions, and More...

Focaccia bread is best when fresh; for refrigerated or frozen focaccia, use the following method to reheat: Preheat oven to 375°F. Place uncut focaccia loaf on a baking sheet and sprinkle with a few drops of water to help rehydrate. For refrigerated or stale focaccia, bake 6–8 minutes until warmed through and crispy. For frozen focaccia, wrap the loaf in aluminum foil and bake 12 minutes. Remove foil and bake an additional 2 minutes to crisp up the crust.

Chopped Italian Sub Bowl

SERVES 4

Quickly combine all of the ingredients and flavors you love from an Italian sub sandwich without the bread for a delicious and satisfying lower-carb dinner. If you miss the bread, add croutons or serve a hunk of baguette on the side. For extra pizzazz and a bit of heat, top the salad with chopped mild or hot cherry peppers.

PREP TIME: 15 MINUTES • ACTIVE COOK TIME: N/A • HANDS-OFF COOK TIME: N/A

3 tablespoons avocado oil

1 tablespoon red wine vinegar

1 teaspoon dried oregano

1/2 teaspoon kosher salt

1/4 teaspoon ground black pepper

4 (1-ounce) slices provolone cheese

4 ounces sliced ham

2 ounces sliced Genoa salami

2 ounces sliced pepperoni

8 ounces grape tomatoes, halved from top to bottom

1/2 small sweet onion, peeled and thinly sliced

1 (8-ounce) bag shredded iceberg lettuce

1 In a large mixing bowl, combine oil, vinegar, oregano, salt, and pepper; set aside.

2 On a cutting board, stack cheese, ham, salami, and pepperoni. Use a chefs knife to cut the stack into 1" cubes. Don't bother separating and toss into mixing bowl with dressing.

3 Add tomatoes, onion, and lettuce. Toss until all ingredients are well coated and serve immediately.

PER SERVING
Calories: 382 | Fat: 30g | Protein: 23g | Sodium: 960mg | Fiber: 1g | Carbohydrates: 5g | Sugar: 1g

Za'atar-Spiced Chicken Salad Pita Pockets

SERVES
4

These pita pockets are loaded with a zesty za'atar-spiced tahini dressing tossed with rotisserie chicken and a few spices. Stuff into fresh pita breads with sliced tomato, cucumber, and onion and enjoy an easy and delicious dinner in minutes!

PREP TIME: 15 MINUTES ● ACTIVE COOK TIME: N/A ● HANDS-OFF COOK TIME: N/A

1/4 cup tahini

2 tablespoons extra-virgin olive oil

Juice of 1 medium lemon

1 tablespoon za'atar

1/2 teaspoon kosher salt

1/4 teaspoons ground black pepper

12 ounces shredded or cubed rotisserie chicken

4 pita breads, sliced open

1 large beefsteak tomato, cut into 8 slices

1/2 medium English cucumber, cut into 8 slices

1/2 small sweet onion, peeled and cut into 4 slices

1 In a large mixing bowl, whisk together tahini, oil, lemon juice, za'atar, salt, and pepper. Add warm water to thin out if needed, adding 1 tablespoon at a time and whisking completely before adding any additional water, until sauce is easy to mix but still thick enough to cling to a spoon.

2 Stir in chicken and mix until well coated by tahini dressing.

3 Fill each pita with equal amounts chicken salad, tomato, cucumber, and onion. Serve.

PER SERVING
Calories: 551 | Fat: 25g | Protein: 27g | Sodium: 1,082mg | Fiber: 9g | Carbohydrates: 54g | Sugar: 4g

Tips, Substitutions, and More...

For a kick of heat, add 1/2 teaspoon crushed red pepper flakes or 1 tablespoon of your favorite hot sauce to the dressing before adding the chicken. For a low-carb and gluten-free option, skip the pita bread and use lettuce leaves as wraps.

CHAPTER FIVE

CONVENIENT CASSEROLES

85

Convenient casseroles are exactly what you will get when you decide what to make for dinner from this chapter. You will find that all of the casserole recipes are one-dish baked dinners that will be easy and quick to assemble, with the majority of the cooking as hands-off cook time. Long gone are the days of mushy vegetables, chemical-laden soups as casserole starters, and a hodgepodge of leftover ingredients. All of the following recipes deliver modern and ridiculously easy complete dinners that are not only cooked in a casserole dish but mostly prepped and assembled in the very same casserole dish.

Whip up delicious recipes like Deconstructed Chicken Cordon Bleu Casserole surrounded by quick-cooking fresh green beans, Cheater Chicken "Tender" Parmesan (featuring high-quality frozen breaded chicken tenders to avoid having to cut, pound, bread, and fry chicken cutlets), and Chile Rellenos Casserole with Chorizo that rivals its deep-fried counterpart.

Artichoke Dip Chicken and Rice Casserole

SERVES 6

This recipe is a modern take that combines two popular dishes: artichoke dip and chicken and rice casserole. Don't swap in fresh spinach for frozen: The extra water that the frozen spinach releases is accounted for in the recipe and necessary to create the sauce and properly cook the rice.

PREP TIME: 15 MINUTES • ACTIVE COOK TIME: N/A • HANDS-OFF COOK TIME: 90 MINUTES

1½ cups low-sodium chicken broth

1 cup half-and-half

4 cloves garlic, peeled and crushed

¾ teaspoon kosher salt

½ teaspoon ground black pepper

½ teaspoon paprika

1 (12-ounce) jar marinated and quartered artichokes, drained (8 ounces drained)

1 (8-ounce) bag frozen chopped spinach

1 cup uncooked jasmine rice, rinsed

2 (5.2-ounce) packages Boursin Garlic & Fine Herbs cheese

1½ pounds boneless, skinless chicken breast, cut into 1" chunks

1 cup grated Parmesan cheese

1 cup panko bread crumbs

1 Preheat oven to 400°F.

2 In a 9" × 13" casserole dish, combine broth, half-and-half, garlic, spices, artichokes, and spinach until well mixed.

3 Add rice, using a spoon to push down so that all rice grains are submerged under broth mixture. Crumble both containers of Boursin cheese over the mixture. Add chicken, taking care that chicken pieces are at least half submerged.

4 Cover tightly with aluminum foil and bake undisturbed 60 minutes.

5 In a small bowl, combine Parmesan and panko and set aside.

6 Remove foil, stir ingredients to mix well, and flatten out top. Top casserole with Parmesan and panko mixture and spray evenly with nonstick cooking spray. Bake uncovered an additional 30 minutes.

7 Remove from oven and allow to rest 5 minutes before serving.

PER SERVING
Calories: 712 | Fat: 39g | Protein: 42g | Sodium: 1,564mg | Fiber: 4g | Carbohydrates: 48g | Sugar: 4g

Vegetarian Pesto Lazy Lasagna

SERVES 8

The most time-consuming part of making a homemade lasagna is precooking all of the ingredients such as parboiling noodles and sautéing vegetables to sweat out the excess liquid. This Vegetarian Pesto Lazy Lasagna uses multiple prep and assembly shortcuts as well as accounting for the excess water from the frozen greens and raw mushrooms as part of the recipe to eliminate any precooking.

PREP TIME: 15 MINUTES • ACTIVE COOK TIME: N/A • HANDS-OFF COOK TIME: 90 MINUTES

1 (16-ounce) container full-fat ricotta cheese

3/4 cup basil pesto

1 large egg

2 (24-ounce) jars marinara sauce

8 ounces uncooked no-boil lasagna noodles

1 (16-ounce) bag frozen chopped spinach

1 (10-ounce) package sliced white mushrooms

16 ounces shredded mozzarella cheese

6 ounces grated Parmesan cheese

1/2 cup finely chopped fresh basil

1 Preheat oven to 350°F.

2 In a small bowl, combine ricotta, pesto, and egg. Set aside.

3 Spray a 9" × 13" casserole dish with nonstick cooking spray. Spread 1/2 cup marinara on the bottom of the casserole dish. Add single layer of noodles (it's okay to break them to fit).

4 Spread 1/3 of ricotta mixture on noodles. Top with 1/3 of frozen spinach and 1/3 of mushrooms.

5 Sprinkle with 1/4 of mozzarella and 1/4 of Parmesan. Repeat layers two more times, reserving 1 cup marinara for top layer and adding the rest in middle layer.

6 Tear off a piece of aluminum foil large enough to cover lasagna and spray one side with nonstick cooking spray. Cover lasagna tightly with foil, spray side down. Place casserole dish on a baking sheet and bake on center rack 45 minutes.

Continued ▶

7 Carefully remove foil (if any cheese sticks, use a butter knife to scrape off and place back on top of lasagna). Return to oven and bake uncovered an additional 45 minutes.

8 Remove from oven and allow lasagna to cool 10 minutes. When ready to serve, sprinkle with chopped basil and cut.

PER SERVING
Calories: 610 | Fat: 31g | Protein: 37g | Sodium: 1,535mg | Fiber: 9g | Carbohydrates: 46g | Sugar: 7g

Tips, Substitutions, and More...

If you want to add meat without any additional work, tuck mini pepperoni rounds into the layers before adding the vegetables. Frozen chopped broccoli rabe can be substituted for frozen spinach.

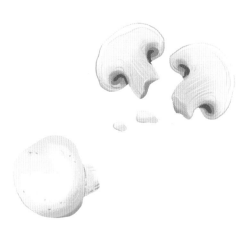

Deconstructed Chicken Cordon Bleu Casserole

SERVES 6

This take on chicken cordon bleu eliminates all of the time-consuming prep work usually involved. Skip pounding out chicken cutlets, breading, stuffing, and deep-frying and instead assemble everything in a mere 10 minutes and bake for just half an hour.

PREP TIME: 10 MINUTES • ACTIVE COOK TIME: N/A • HANDS-OFF COOK TIME: 30 MINUTES

2 tablespoons extra-virgin olive oil

1 (12-ounce) package cleaned and trimmed green beans

1 teaspoon kosher salt, divided

1 teaspoon ground black pepper, divided

6 boneless, skinless chicken cutlets (or 3 breasts cut horizontally into 6 cutlets), about 2^{1}/$_{4}$ pounds

2 tablespoons Dijon mustard

1 teaspoon dried parsley

6 (1-ounce) slices ham

6 ounces shredded Swiss cheese

4 tablespoons salted butter

1 cup panko bread crumbs

1 Preheat oven to 450°F.

2 In a 9" × 13" casserole dish, add oil and green beans. Sprinkle ^{1}/$_{2}$ teaspoon salt and ^{1}/$_{2}$ teaspoon pepper over green beans. Toss until well coated with oil and spices.

3 Add chicken to casserole dish in a single layer over green beans. Use a spoon to spread mustard over chicken cutlets. Sprinkle remaining ^{1}/$_{2}$ teaspoon salt, remaining ^{1}/$_{2}$ teaspoon pepper, and parsley over chicken.

4 Place 1 slice ham on top of each chicken cutlet and top each with 1 ounce cheese.

5 Place butter in a microwave-safe measuring cup or mug and melt (20–30 seconds) on high. Remove from microwave and stir in panko. Stir until butter is completely absorbed and panko is well coated.

6 Evenly sprinkle buttered panko over top of cheese. Cover casserole dish with aluminum foil. Bake on center rack 15 minutes.

7 Remove foil and bake uncovered an additional 15 minutes or until cheese is melted and panko is beginning to brown. Remove from oven and cool 5 minutes before serving.

PER SERVING
Calories: 481 | Fat: 25g | Protein: 50g | Sodium: 822mg | Fiber: 2g | Carbohydrates: 13g | Sugar: 2g

Cheater Chicken "Tender" Parmesan

Use high-quality frozen, breaded chicken tenders or nuggets to make the quickest chicken parmesan you will ever have. Serve alongside baby arugula simply dressed with olive oil, balsamic vinegar, salt, and pepper for an unforgettable family meal that everyone will love.

PREP TIME: 5 MINUTES • ACTIVE COOK TIME: N/A • HANDS-OFF COOK TIME: 40 MINUTES

24 ounces frozen, breaded chicken tenders or nuggets

1/2 teaspoon Italian seasoning

1/4 teaspoon kosher salt

1/8 teaspoon ground black pepper

2 cups shredded mozzarella cheese, divided

1/2 cup Parmesan cheese, divided

1 (24-ounce) jar marinara sauce, divided

1 Preheat oven to 375°F. Spray a 9" × 13" casserole dish with nonstick cooking spray.

2 Layer chicken tenders in casserole dish. Sprinkle with Italian seasoning, salt, and pepper.

3 Sprinkle 1 cup mozzarella and 1/4 cup Parmesan on top. Pour all of the marinara sauce except 1/2 cup over chicken. Finish with remaining mozzarella and Parmesan.

4 Cover tightly with aluminum foil and bake on center rack 30 minutes.

5 Remove foil and bake an additional 10 minutes or until the cheese is bubbling and beginning to brown. Allow to cool 10 minutes before serving. Warm reserved marinara sauce in microwave on high 20 seconds, then serve on the side.

Tips, Substitutions, and More...

High-quality breaded chicken tender brands include Bell & Evans and Applegate.

PER SERVING
Calories: 369 | Fat: 14g | Protein: 33g | Sodium: 1,148mg | Fiber: 3g | Carbohydrates: 27g | Sugar: 7g

Foolproof Roast Chicken with Pearl Potatoes

SERVES 6

Making a whole chicken with this easy technique is foolproof! The chicken cooks on top of the vegetables and potatoes, which adds so much flavor. Cooking a whole chicken in a shallow casserole dish allows air to circulate around the skin and ensure it gets crispy. The key to saving time is to look for pearl potatoes, also called peewee, creamer, or two-bite potatoes; they are so small they don't need any prep work other than a rinse.

PREP TIME: 10 MINUTES ● ACTIVE COOK TIME: N/A ● HANDS-OFF COOK TIME: 90 MINUTES

1 1/2 teaspoons kosher salt

1 1/2 teaspoons paprika

1 teaspoon dried parsley

1 teaspoon dried thyme

2 pounds pearl potatoes

4 medium carrots, peeled and cut into 3" chunks

1 large yellow onion, peeled and cut into 8 wedges

1/4 cup extra-virgin olive oil, divided

1 (4-pound) whole chicken

Tips, Substitutions, and More...

If you can't find pearl potatoes, you can substitute quartered Yukon Gold potatoes (unpeeled). To save even more time, swap 1/2 pound of baby carrots for the regular carrots.

1 Preheat oven to 425°F.

2 In a small dish, mix salt and spices together and set aside.

3 In a 9" × 13" casserole dish, combine potatoes, carrots, onion, 3 tablespoons oil, and half of spice mixture.

4 Place chicken breast side down in dish. Drizzle 1/2 tablespoon oil and half of remaining spice mixture over chicken. Bake on center rack 30 minutes.

5 Remove from oven. Use strong tongs to lift chicken onto a dinner plate. Use a large spoon or spatula to toss vegetables.

6 Return chicken to casserole dish breast side up. Drizzle remaining 1/2 tablespoon oil and spice mixture over chicken. Bake 60 minutes.

7 Remove from oven and transfer chicken to a cutting board to carve. Serve alongside cooked potatoes, carrots, and onion.

PER SERVING
Calories: 574 | Fat: 15g | Protein: 59g | Sodium: 831mg | Fiber: 5g | Carbohydrates: 51g | Sugar: 13g

Mediterranean-Inspired Orzo, Chicken, and Boursin

SERVES
6

This modern take on the classic chicken, broccoli, and rice casserole combines quick-cooking orzo pasta, flavor-packed sun-dried tomatoes, chicken, broccoli florets, and garlic-herb Boursin cheese for a delicious meal that only takes 15 minutes of active prep time.

PREP TIME: 15 MINUTES • ACTIVE COOK TIME: N/A • HANDS-OFF COOK TIME: 60 MINUTES

4 cups low-sodium chicken broth

1 teaspoon Italian seasoning

1 teaspoon kosher salt

1/2 teaspoon ground black pepper

1/4 teaspoon crushed red pepper flakes

1/2 cup sun-dried tomatoes in oil, drained with 1/4 cup oil reserved

6 cloves garlic, peeled and crushed

2 cups uncooked orzo pasta

1 1/2 pounds boneless, skinless chicken breast, cut into 1" chunks

1 (12-ounce) bag fresh broccoli florets

2 (5.2-ounce) packages Boursin Garlic & Fine Herbs cheese

1 cup (about 2 1/2 ounces) grated Parmesan cheese

1 Preheat oven to 425°F.

2 In a 9" × 13" casserole dish, combine broth, spices, sun-dried tomatoes and oil, garlic, and orzo. Add chicken and broccoli, taking care to make sure that the orzo remains submerged under the seasoned broth.

3 Place both packages of Boursin cheese on top of orzo mixture, one on each side of the casserole, and gently push down. Cover with aluminum foil and bake on center rack 45 minutes.

4 Remove foil and stir until well mixed. Top with Parmesan and bake uncovered 15 minutes. Serve.

PER SERVING
Calories: 730 | Fat: 29g | Protein: 47g | Sodium: 1,033mg | Fiber: 4g | Carbohydrates: 70g | Sugar: 10g

Shortcut Ravioli and Italian Sausage "Lasagna"

Use fresh or frozen regular-sized ravioli to create a soul-warming meat- and vegetable-loaded "lasagna" in just 5 minutes of prep time, eliminating almost all of the typical lasagna assembly work. Combine the ravioli with uncooked crumbled Italian sausage, high-quality jarred marinara sauce, and shredded cheese in layers, bake, then enjoy!

PREP TIME: 5 MINUTES • ACTIVE COOK TIME: N/A • HANDS-OFF COOK TIME: 60 MINUTES

2 (24-ounce) jars marinara sauce

1 (24-ounce) package spinach and cheese ravioli

1 pound bulk uncooked mild Italian sausage, crumbled

3 cups (12 ounces) shredded mozzarella cheese

1 cup (3 ounces) grated or shredded Parmesan cheese

Tips, Substitutions, and More...

Spinach and cheese ravioli means a nice serving of vegetables, but you can substitute plain cheese ravioli or experiment with almost any other type of fresh or frozen standard-sized ravioli without changing the cooking time. For a bit of heat, substitute spicy Italian sausage, or sprinkle with crushed red pepper flakes before cutting and serving.

1 Preheat oven to 400°F.

2 Spread 1/2 cup marinara sauce on bottom of an ungreased 9" × 13" casserole dish. Layer half of ravioli on sauce. Top with half of sausage. Sprinkle on 1 cup mozzarella and 1/3 cup Parmesan. Repeat with a layer of half of remaining sauce, remaining ravioli, remaining sausage, and half of remaining cheeses. Top with remaining sauce and cheeses.

3 Cover tightly with aluminum foil and bake on center rack 45 minutes.

4 Remove foil and bake uncovered an additional 15 minutes or until cheese is bubbly and begins to brown.

5 Remove from oven and allow to rest 15 minutes before cutting and serving.

PER SERVING
Calories: 464 | Fat: 27g | Protein: 25g | Sodium: 1,458mg | Fiber: 3g | Carbohydrates: 30g | Sugar: 10g

Asparagus, Turkey Sausage, and Gouda Savory Strata

SERVES 6

This savory strata combines the goodness of already cooked sausage, shredded Gouda cheese, fresh asparagus, a bit of onion, and cubed sourdough with eggs and seasonings for a hearty meal loaded with flavor and texture. Just 15 minutes of prep work and assembly and the oven does the rest of the work!

PREP TIME: 15 MINUTES ● ACTIVE COOK TIME: N/A ● HANDS-OFF COOK TIME: 60 MINUTES

6 large eggs

2 cups whole milk

1 1/2 teaspoons kosher salt

1/2 teaspoon ground black pepper

1/2 teaspoon dried parsley

1/2 teaspoon paprika

1 (12-ounce) sourdough baguette, cut into 1" cubes

1 (12-ounce) package fully cooked turkey sausage links, quartered and sliced

1 small red onion, peeled, quartered, and thinly sliced

1 small bunch (about 8 ounces) thin asparagus, ends trimmed, cut into 1/2" pieces

1 (8-ounce) package shredded Gouda cheese

Tips, Substitutions, and More...

Any type of cubed crusty bread can substitute for the sourdough baguette. Can't find shredded Gouda? Use shredded Cheddar or Swiss cheese.

1. Preheat oven to 400°F. Spray a 9" × 13" casserole dish with nonstick cooking spray.

2. In casserole dish, combine eggs, milk, and spices. Add cubed baguette and allow to sit in the egg mixture for a few minutes.

3. Stir in sausage, onion, asparagus, and Gouda. Use a spatula to push down ingredients if necessary to make sure that everything is soaked with egg mixture.

4. Tear off a piece of aluminum foil large enough to cover casserole and spray one side with nonstick cooking spray. Place foil spray side down tightly over casserole. Bake on center rack 30 minutes.

5. Carefully remove foil and bake an additional 30 minutes uncovered or until bread has begun to brown and center looks solid. Remove from oven and cool 5 minutes before cutting and serving.

PER SERVING
Calories: 534 | Fat: 26g | Protein: 35g | Sodium: 1,276mg | Fiber: 2g | Carbohydrates: 40g | Sugar: 6g

SERVES 6

Chile Rellenos Casserole with Chorizo

This easy casserole version of chile rellenos combines layers of canned fire-roasted whole chiles, uncooked crumbled chorizo sausage, shredded cheese, and a fluffy egg mixture to create a dish reminiscent of the original dish but without all of the hands-on work required.

PREP TIME: 15 MINUTES • ACTIVE COOK TIME: N/A • HANDS-OFF COOK TIME: 40 MINUTES

8 large eggs

1 cup whole milk

1/2 cup all-purpose flour

1 teaspoon baking powder

1 1/2 teaspoons kosher salt

1/2 teaspoon ground black pepper

1/2 teaspoon smoked paprika

1 (27-ounce) can mild fire-roasted whole green chiles

1 pound bulk uncooked Mexican chorizo sausage, crumbled

2 cups shredded Mexican cheese blend

1 Preheat oven to 375°F. Spray a 9" × 13" casserole dish with nonstick cooking spray.

2 In a large mixing bowl, add eggs, milk, flour, baking powder, salt, pepper, and paprika; whisk until well mixed and eggs are slightly foamy, about 2 minutes.

3 Pour 1 cup of egg mixture into casserole dish and spread around until bottom is covered in a thin layer. Layer half of chiles over egg mixture, splitting each chile open with your fingers so that they lay flat in a single layer. Sprinkle half of chorizo and half of cheese on top. Repeat layering with 1 cup egg mixture and remaining chiles, chorizo, and cheese. Pour remaining egg mixture over top.

4 Bake uncovered on center rack 40 minutes. Remove from oven and allow to rest 5 minutes before cutting and serving.

PER SERVING
Calories: 668 | Fat: 48g | Protein: 40g | Sodium: 1,147mg | Fiber: 4g | Carbohydrates: 19g | Sugar: 6g

Tortellini and Cauliflower– Loaded Pizza Bake

SERVES
6

Use uncooked fresh or frozen cheese tortellini as a base to make a loaded pizza casserole. Get a nice serving of vegetables and add texture by adding cauliflower florets. Next, top the tortellini and cauliflower with marinara sauce, shredded cheese, and the perfect pizza combo of pepperoni, olives, and mushrooms. Save time by using sliced canned olives and look for already sliced mushrooms at the store.

PREP TIME: 5 MINUTES • ACTIVE COOK TIME: N/A • HANDS-OFF COOK TIME: 40 MINUTES

1$\frac{1}{2}$ **pounds uncooked cheese tortellini, frozen or refrigerated**

1 (10-ounce) bag fresh cauliflower florets

1 (24-ounce) jar marinara sauce

$\frac{1}{2}$ **cup water**

3 cups shredded mozzarella cheese, divided

28 mini pepperoni rounds

$\frac{1}{4}$ **cup sliced black olives**

$\frac{1}{2}$ **cup thinly sliced white mushrooms**

Tips, Substitutions, and More...

Do not use frozen cauliflower florets as they will add too much liquid to the casserole and will not have the same texture. When adding the water with the marinara to the casserole, first pour the water into marinara jar, place lid on, and shake to easily get remaining marinara sauce from jar.

1 Preheat oven to 425°F. Spray a 9" × 13" casserole dish with nonstick cooking spray.

2 Pour tortellini and cauliflower florets into casserole dish and spread out in a single layer (as much as possible). Top with marinara and water. Sprinkle 2 cups cheese over casserole and top with pepperoni, olives, and mushrooms. Sprinkle remaining 1 cup cheese over casserole.

3 Bake uncovered on center rack 40 minutes or until cheese is completely melted and brown around edges.

4 Remove from oven and allow to rest 5 minutes before serving.

PER SERVING
Calories: 689 | Fat: 26g | Protein: 34g | Sodium: 1,090mg | Fiber: 3g | Carbohydrates: 80g | Sugar: 7g

Meatloaf Casserole with Tater Tot Topping

SERVES
8

Save time by using the casserole dish to create the meatloaf mixture right in the dish—no need for another mixing bowl. And, no need to form or shape a meatloaf, just press into the dish and flatten. Top with a bit of ketchup and frozen Tater Tots, then let the oven do the rest of the work. Comfort food casserole incoming in 60 minutes!

PREP TIME: 15 MINUTES ● ACTIVE COOK TIME: N/A ● HANDS-OFF COOK TIME: 60 MINUTES

$1^1/_2$ cups plain bread crumbs

1 cup whole milk

2 teaspoons kosher salt

1 teaspoon dried parsley

$^1/_2$ teaspoon ground black pepper

$^1/_4$ teaspoon onion powder

$^1/_3$ cup plus $^1/_4$ cup ketchup, divided

$^1/_4$ cup Worcestershire sauce

2 large eggs

2 pounds 80% lean ground beef

$1^1/_2$ pounds frozen Tater Tots

1 Preheat oven to 400°F.

2 In a 9" × 13" casserole dish, use a fork to combine bread crumbs, milk, salt, parsley, pepper, and onion powder until well mixed. Allow mixture to sit 5 minutes for bread crumb mixture to absorb liquid from milk.

3 Add $^1/_3$ cup ketchup, Worcestershire sauce, and eggs to bread crumb mixture. Use a fork to mix until well combined. Add in ground beef and use your hands to fold beef into bread crumb mixture until just combined. Pack mixture evenly into the casserole dish so that there is no space. Use a spoon to evenly spread remaining $^1/_4$ cup ketchup over top of meatloaf.

4 Arrange Tater Tots in a single layer over meatloaf, gently pressing down each Tater Tot. Bake uncovered on center rack 55–60 minutes until Tater Tots are brown and sides of meatloaf are bubbling.

5 Remove from oven and cool at least 10 minutes before cutting and serving.

PER SERVING
Calories: 575 | Fat: 33g | Protein: 27g | Sodium: 1,276mg | Fiber: 3g | Carbohydrates: 43g | Sugar: 9g

Cabbage Roll Casserole

Classic cabbage rolls are a family favorite (and usually a labor of love). First you have to blanch the cabbage leaves, then cook rice and separately sauté a ground beef and rice mixture. Not to mention the time it takes to assemble the rolls or make the simmering sauce. This simple casserole version eliminates all of that work and delivers on a dish that has the familiar flavors you love.

PREP TIME: 15 MINUTES • ACTIVE COOK TIME: N/A • HANDS-OFF COOK TIME: 90 MINUTES

2 tablespoons extra-virgin olive oil

1½ pounds 80% lean ground beef

1 large yellow onion, peeled, halved, and thinly sliced

4 cloves garlic, peeled and crushed

1 tablespoon granulated sugar

2½ teaspoons kosher salt

1 teaspoon paprika

1 teaspoon dried parsley

½ teaspoon ground black pepper

1 cup uncooked jasmine rice, rinsed

2 (15-ounce) cans tomato sauce

1¾ cups low-sodium chicken broth

2½ pounds green cabbage, cut into 1" chunks

1 Preheat oven to 350°F.

2 In a 9" × 13" casserole dish, combine oil, ground beef, onion, garlic, sugar, salt, spices, and rice. Pour over tomato sauce and then broth. Don't stir but push down any rice that isn't in liquid. Top with cabbage. The mixture will be a mound that may seem like too much for the casserole dish, but it will shrink significantly as it cooks. Just push down the cabbage and cover tightly with aluminum foil.

3 Place casserole on a baking sheet and bake on center rack undisturbed 60 minutes.

4 Remove from oven, carefully remove foil, stir until cabbage is well combined into mixture, and make sure that any uncooked rice is submerged in remaining liquid. Re-cover and bake an additional 30 minutes.

5 Remove from oven, remove foil, and allow to sit 5 minutes before serving.

PER SERVING
Calories: 573 | Fat: 28g | Protein: 27g | Sodium: 1,324mg | Fiber: 6g | Carbohydrates: 53g | Sugar: 16g

CHAPTER SIX

SHEET PAN DINNERS

103

Create an entire meal on a rimmed baking sheet, otherwise known as a sheet pan! In this chapter, you'll learn how to make Sheet Pan Shrimp Scampi with Broccoli and Garlic Bread in just 30 minutes, and Pesto Lovers' Sliders with Turkey, Provolone, and Roasted Peppers to feed a crowd. You'll also find out how to hack making Fish Stick Tacos with Shredded Cabbage by using crunchy breaded fish sticks, and more.

Many of the recipes for sheet pan dinners in this book call for using parchment paper to expedite cleanup. Don't skip this step or you will wind up having to soak your sheet pan and add unnecessary cleanup time. When it comes to getting the parchment paper to stay on the tray without slipping around, a quick tip is to cut the piece of parchment paper a little larger than the size of your sheet pan, then crumble it into a ball. Unfold the ball and place the paper on the baking sheet. All of the new crinkles and ridges will prevent the parchment from moving around.

Cheesy Baked Refried Bean Tacos

SERVES
4

In just 15 minutes, you can have an entire sheet pan–sized tray of warm tacos that the whole family will love. For this easy recipe, canned refried beans are used to eliminate the need to precook any other types of protein. Just add cheese, bake, and serve with your favorite toppings!

PREP TIME: 8 MINUTES • ACTIVE COOK TIME: N/A • HANDS-OFF COOK TIME: 7 MINUTES

12 hard-shell corn taco shells

1 (16-ounce) can traditional refried beans

6 ounces shredded Mexican cheese blend

1 (8-ounce) bag shredded iceberg lettuce

4 ounces full-fat sour cream

4 ounces pico de gallo

1 Preheat oven to 375°F. Line an 18" × 13" rimmed sheet pan with parchment paper.

2 Spread out taco shells on sheet. Gently fill each taco shell with approximately 1 heaping tablespoon refried beans. Next, sprinkle cheese into taco shells.

3 Bake on center rack 7 minutes.

4 Remove and serve with lettuce, sour cream, and pico de gallo on the side.

PER SERVING
Calories: 349 | Fat: 20g | Protein: 17g | Sodium: 720mg | Fiber: 5g | Carbohydrates: 25g | Sugar: 5g

Tips, Substitutions, and More…

Many brands of traditional refried beans contain lard. For a vegetarian option, swap in vegetarian refried black or pinto beans. For heat, add hot sauce or pickled jalapeños on the side when serving. Shredded green or red cabbage or even slaw mix can replace the shredded lettuce.

Sheet Pan Shrimp Scampi with Broccoli and Garlic Bread

SERVES
4

Get ready to impress! This gourmet dinner only takes 10 minutes of prep time by using already peeled and deveined fresh shrimp (or defrosted peeled and deveined shrimp from the freezer). Combined with roasted broccoli and crispy garlic bread, this is a simple meal you will want to enjoy on repeat.

PREP TIME: 10 MINUTES ● ACTIVE COOK TIME: N/A ● HANDS-OFF COOK TIME: 20 MINUTES

For Broccoli

1 (1-pound) bag fresh broccoli florets

2 tablespoons extra-virgin olive oil

1/2 teaspoon kosher salt

1/4 teaspoon ground black pepper

1/4 teaspoon crushed red pepper flakes

1 To make Broccoli: Preheat oven to 425°F and line an 18" × 13" rimmed sheet pan with parchment paper.

2 Add all ingredients to sheet and toss until well coated. Bake on center rack 10 minutes.

For Garlic Butter

4 tablespoons salted butter, melted

2 tablespoons extra-virgin olive oil

4 cloves garlic, peeled and crushed

1 tablespoon dried parsley

1 teaspoon kosher salt

1/2 teaspoon ground black pepper

1/4 teaspoon crushed red pepper flakes

3 To make Garlic Butter: Add butter to a glass measuring cup with oil, garlic, and spices. Stir to mix and set aside.

For Shrimp and Garlic Bread

1 (6-ounce) white baguette, cut in half lengthwise and then horizontally

1¹/2 pounds fresh, uncooked, peeled, deveined large shrimp, patted dry

4 tablespoons grated Parmesan cheese

1 medium lemon, halved

4 To make Shrimp and Garlic Bread: Remove sheet pan with broccoli to a heat-safe surface. Use a spatula to move partially cooked broccoli to the middle ¹/3 of sheet.

5 Arrange sliced baguette on left ¹/3 of sheet, cut side up. Arrange shrimp on right ¹/3 of sheet, in a single layer (close together is fine).

6 Spoon 1 tablespoon Garlic Butter over each piece of baguette. Spoon remaining Garlic Butter over shrimp. Sprinkle 1 tablespoon Parmesan over each piece of baguette.

7 Bake on center rack 10 minutes or until garlic bread is toasted and shrimp are cooked through.

8 Remove from oven and squeeze lemon over shrimp and broccoli. Serve immediately.

PER SERVING
Calories: 530 | Fat: 30g | Protein: 32g | Sodium: 1,562mg | Fiber: 0g | Carbohydrates: 34g | Sugar: 0g

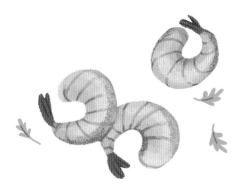

Curried Chickpeas with No-Prep Vegetables

SERVES 4

This weeknight vegetarian dinner of curried chickpeas with no-prep convenience vegetables comes together in just minutes. The aromatic spice mixture infuses the chickpeas, cauliflower florets, and green beans, creating a flavor-packed meal that is excellent served with reheated rice or warmed-up naan bread.

PREP TIME: 5 MINUTES • ACTIVE COOK TIME: N/A • HANDS-OFF COOK TIME: 25 MINUTES

1/4 cup avocado oil

1 tablespoon curry powder

1 teaspoon kosher salt

1/2 teaspoon ground ginger

1/4 teaspoon ground black pepper

1/4 teaspoon cayenne pepper

4 cloves garlic, peeled and crushed

2 (15-ounce) cans chickpeas, drained and rinsed

1 (12-ounce) bag fresh cauliflower florets

6 ounces cleaned and trimmed green beans

1 Preheat oven to 450°F.

2 While oven preheats, add all ingredients to a large mixing bowl and toss until well coated.

3 Spread ingredients onto an unlined 18" × 13" rimmed sheet pan in a single layer. Bake 25 minutes, gently tossing mixture one time halfway through cooking. Serve.

PER SERVING
Calories: 338 | Fat: 18g | Protein: 12g | Sodium: 876mg |
Fiber: 12g | Carbohydrates: 32g | Sugar: 3g

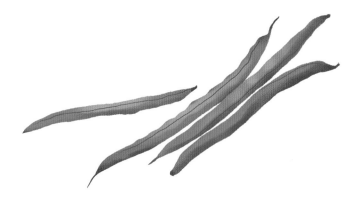

Fish Stick Tacos with Shredded Cabbage

SERVES
4

In the mood for fish tacos but want to avoid the steps of preparing the fish, dipping it into batter, frying it, and cleaning up? Skip all of the extra work by using crunchy, frozen, breaded fish sticks to make amazing fish tacos in minutes!

PREP TIME: 5 MINUTES • ACTIVE COOK TIME: N/A • HANDS-OFF COOK TIME: 20 MINUTES

24 frozen breaded fish sticks

1 (8-ounce) bag shredded cabbage

2 medium avocados, peeled, pitted, and sliced

3 limes, cut into quarters

8 ounces pico de gallo

12 (6") flour tortillas

1 Preheat oven to 425°F. Line an 18" × 13" rimmed sheet pan with parchment paper.

2 Arrange fish sticks in a single layer on sheet and bake on center rack 20 minutes (or according to package instructions), flipping one time, or until crispy.

3 While baking fish sticks, set out cabbage, avocado, limes, and pico de gallo.

4 Stack flour tortillas and wrap tightly in aluminum foil. Add foil-wrapped stack of tortillas to oven for the last 8 minutes of cooking time to heat through.

5 Serve each tortilla filled with 2 fish sticks, cabbage, avocado, pico de gallo, and a squeeze of lime.

Tips, Substitutions, and More...

Look for 100% wild-caught fish sticks that have a crunchy-style breading to mimic fried fish for fish tacos. Substitute slaw mix or shredded iceberg lettuce for shredded cabbage if preferred. Additional optional topping ideas include: sour cream, pickled jalapeños, sliced or diced red onion, cilantro leaves, hot sauce, and guacamole.

PER SERVING
Calories: 694 | Fat: 32g | Protein: 27g | Sodium: 761mg | Fiber: 10g | Carbohydrates: 75g | Sugar: 4g

Pesto-Crusted Cod with Sugar Snap Peas and Delicata Squash

SERVES 4

This creative sheet pan dinner features cod fillets generously coated with a flavorful pesto crust, served alongside simply prepared crisp sugar snap peas and tender delicata squash with crispy edges. Save even more time by looking in the refrigerated convenience vegetable section for a container or bag of already cleaned and cut delicata squash rings!

PREP TIME: 10 MINUTES • ACTIVE COOK TIME: N/A • HANDS-OFF COOK TIME: 40 MINUTES

1 pound delicata squash, sliced in half from top to bottom, seeds removed, cut into 1/2"-thick half-moons

2 tablespoons extra-virgin olive oil

1 teaspoon kosher salt

4 (6-ounce, 1"-thick) wild cod fillets, patted dry

4 tablespoons basil pesto

4 tablespoons panko bread crumbs

Avocado oil cooking spray

1 (12-ounce) package sugar snap peas

Tips, Substitutions, and More...

Fish should flake apart easily from the center or be at 145°F internal temperature. These instructions are for 1"-thick pieces. You may need to decrease or increase fish cooking time based on thickness if you don't use 1" pieces.

1 Preheat oven to 425°F. Line an 18" × 13" rimmed baking sheet with parchment paper.

2 Add squash pieces to lined sheet pan. Toss with oil and salt. Spread out in a single layer, place in oven on center rack, and bake undisturbed 25 minutes.

3 Remove from oven, then flip squash pieces and push off to 1/3 of sheet to make room for cod and snap peas.

4 Add cod pieces to the middle 1/3 of sheet. Top each piece with 1 tablespoon pesto, 1 tablespoon panko, and finish with avocado oil spray. Return sheet to oven and bake 10 minutes.

5 Remove sheet and add snap peas to the empty section. Toss with avocado oil spray. Place sheet back into oven and bake 5 more minutes. Serve immediately.

PER SERVING
Calories: 326 | Fat: 16g | Protein: 27g | Sodium: 708mg | Fiber: 4g | Carbohydrates: 17g | Sugar: 7g

Tandoori-Spiced Salmon with Potatoes and Green Beans

SERVES 4

Use premade tandoori masala spice mix to create a flavor-packed dinner of salmon, potatoes, and green beans in no time. Premade tandoori seasoning is often called "tandoori masala" and can typically be found in the spice aisle or in the specialty food aisle of your grocery store.

PREP TIME: 10 MINUTES • ACTIVE COOK TIME: N/A • HANDS-OFF COOK TIME: 32 MINUTES

1 pound small butter potatoes, quartered

¼ cup extra-virgin olive oil

3 tablespoons tandoori seasoning

1 (12-ounce) package cleaned and trimmed green beans

4 (6-ounce) wild Alaskan salmon fillets

Tips, Substitutions, and More...

To keep your prep time to a minimum, make sure to buy already cleaned and trimmed green beans in the refrigerated vegetable section of your grocery store. If the spice mix is salt-free, add 1 teaspoon kosher salt to the mixture. To add a kick of heat, add ½ teaspoon cayenne pepper. Optional: Serve with lemon slices and a dollop of full-fat plain yogurt on the side for extra pizzazz.

1 Preheat oven to 425°F. Line an 18" × 13" rimmed baking sheet pan with parchment paper.

2 On lined sheet pan, combine potatoes, oil, and tandoori seasoning until well coated. Push potatoes to the side and toss green beans in remaining seasoned oil on sheet.

3 Remove green beans to a dinner plate.

4 Rub both sides of salmon fillets in remaining seasoned oil and place salmon on dinner plate with green beans.

5 Space out potatoes on sheet and bake 20 minutes.

6 Remove from oven. Use a spatula to make space between the potatoes and add green beans and salmon, skin side down. Return sheet to oven and bake an additional 10–12 minutes until salmon reaches 130°F–140°F (closer to 130°F for a creamier texture).

7 Divide onto four dinner plates and serve.

PER SERVING

Calories: 492 | Fat: 26g | Protein: 39g | Sodium: 100mg | Fiber: 4g | Carbohydrates: 25g | Sugar: 4g

Copycat Barbecue Chicken Naan Pizza

SERVES 4

While there are many copycat versions of barbecue naan pizza out there, this one has only 10 minutes of prep time. It utilizes rotisserie chicken, shredded cheese, fresh or frozen naan bread (same cooking time!), and a bit of red onion and pickled jalapeños for a bit of acid and heat.

PREP TIME: 10 MINUTES • ACTIVE COOK TIME: N/A • HANDS-OFF COOK TIME: 16 MINUTES

4 naan breads, fresh or frozen

1/2 cup plus 4 teaspoons Kansas City–style barbecue sauce, divided

1 cup (about 6 ounces) shredded mozzarella cheese, divided

1 cup (about 6 ounces) shredded or chopped rotisserie chicken

1/4 small red onion, peeled, halved, and thinly sliced

20 pickled sliced jalapeños

1 Preheat oven to 425°F. Line an 18" × 13" rimmed sheet pan with parchment paper and place naan on sheet.

2 Evenly divide 1/2 cup barbecue sauce onto naan and spread out, leaving a thin border.

3 Next, sprinkle 1/2 cup mozzarella onto naan. Top with chicken, onion, and jalapeños.

4 Finish with remaining mozzarella and drizzle with remaining barbecue sauce.

5 Bake on center rack 14–16 minutes until cheese begins to bubble and is slightly brown. Serve.

PER SERVING
Calories: 523 | Fat: 19g | Protein: 28g | Sodium: 1,031mg | Fiber: 3g | Carbohydrates: 60g | Sugar: 13g

Spiced Chicken Thighs with Chickpeas, Fennel, and Olives

Combine boneless, skinless chicken thighs with canned chickpeas, pitted olives, fennel slices, and a mix of olive oil and tandoori seasoning for a quick and easy sheet pan dinner that is loaded with flavor. Serve with a squeeze of lemon and some warmed naan bread from the freezer.

PREP TIME: 10 MINUTES ● ACTIVE COOK TIME: N/A ● HANDS-OFF COOK TIME: 30 MINUTES

$1\frac{1}{2}$ **pounds boneless, skinless chicken thighs**

1 (14-ounce) can chickpeas, drained and rinsed

1 fennel bulb, trimmed of fronds, halved and cut into $\frac{1}{8}$" slices

1 cup pitted kalamata olives, drained

$\frac{1}{4}$ cup extra-virgin olive oil

3 tablespoons tandoori seasoning

4 frozen naan breads

1 medium lemon, quartered

1 Preheat oven to 425°F.

2 Combine chicken, chickpeas, fennel, and olives on an unlined 18" × 13" rimmed sheet pan. Use a few paper towels to pat dry as much moisture as possible. Add oil and tandoori seasoning and toss until everything is well coated.

3 Bake on center rack 30 minutes, flipping everything one time halfway through cooking.

4 Add naan directly to oven rack for the last 4 minutes of cooking time. Serve immediately with lemon on the side for squeezing.

PER SERVING
Calories: 807 | Fat: 43g | Protein: 40g | Sodium: 1,045mg | Fiber: 9g | Carbohydrates: 65g | Sugar: 5g

Tips, Substitutions, and More…

Boneless, skinless chicken tenders can be substituted for the chicken thighs to reduce the cooking time by 8 minutes. If your tandoori seasoning is salt-free, add $\frac{3}{4}$ teaspoon kosher salt to the ingredients on the sheet pan before tossing.

Pesto Lovers' Sliders with Turkey, Provolone, and Roasted Peppers

SERVES 4

A perfect marriage of sweet, savory, and tangy, these Pesto Lovers' Sliders combine melty provolone, warmed-up turkey, and roasted red peppers with a quick pesto butter over the top.

PREP TIME: 10 MINUTES ● ACTIVE COOK TIME: N/A ● HANDS-OFF COOK TIME: 20 MINUTES

1 (12-count) package Hawaiian sweet rolls, loaf intact

1/4 cup plus 2 tablespoons basil pesto, divided

8 (1-ounce) slices provolone cheese

8 (1-ounce) slices deli turkey

4 ounces roasted red peppers in water, drained

2 tablespoons salted butter

1 Preheat oven to 375°F. Line an 18" × 13" rimmed sheet pan with parchment paper.

2 Using a serrated knife, carefully cut the loaf of Hawaiian rolls through the middle into a top and bottom half, keeping the rolls in each half connected.

3 Place bottom section of the rolls (cut side up) onto sheet. Spread 1/4 cup pesto over bottom section of rolls. Evenly arrange 4 slices provolone on top of pesto. Add turkey slices. Use your hands to pull apart the peppers and distribute over turkey. Finish with remaining provolone. Place the top section of rolls cut side down on provolone.

4 Place butter into a small dish or mug and microwave on high 20 seconds. Remove and stir in remaining 2 tablespoons pesto. Pour pesto-butter mixture evenly over the top of sliders. Loosely cover sliders with aluminum foil.

5 Bake on center rack 15 minutes. Remove foil and continue baking an additional 5 minutes.

6 Remove from oven, slice or pull apart, and serve.

Tips, Substitutions, and More...

Substitute shredded mozzarella cheese for sliced provolone if preferred. To add a kick, stir 1/2 teaspoon crushed red pepper flakes into the pesto and butter mixture. For an extra-cheesy version, stir 2 tablespoons grated Parmesan cheese into the pesto-butter mixture.

PER SERVING
Calories: 596 | Fat: 37g | Protein: 34g | Sodium: 1,635mg | Fiber: 3g | Carbohydrates: 30g | Sugar: 9g

Spicy Sausage with Cabbage Wedges and Butter Potatoes

SERVES
4

There is something magical about the combination of sausage, potatoes, and cabbage. This easy sheet pan version has minimal prep time and mostly hands-off cooking time because all you have to do is turn the ingredients one time halfway through cooking. Your house will smell amazing, and your stomach will be even happier!

PREP TIME: 10 MINUTES • ACTIVE COOK TIME: N/A • HANDS-OFF COOK TIME: 60 MINUTES

1 pound small butter potatoes, halved

¼ cup extra-virgin olive oil

1 teaspoon kosher salt

1 teaspoon paprika

½ teaspoon garlic powder

1 medium (about 1.5–2 pounds) head green cabbage, cut into 4 wedges

1½ pounds uncooked spicy Italian sausage links (about 6–8 links)

1 Preheat oven to 425°F.

2 Combine potatoes, oil, and spices on an unlined 18" × 13" rimmed sheet pan. Turn each potato so that it is cut side down.

3 Rub each cabbage wedge (carefully so that they don't fall apart) in leftover seasoned oil on sheet so that each side is coated and place each wedge on sheet.

4 Snuggle sausage links between potatoes and cabbage so that all ingredients are in a single layer. Use a fork to poke two or three holes in each sausage.

5 Bake 60 minutes, removing sheet one time halfway through cook time to flip cabbage, sausages, and potatoes. Serve immediately.

Tips, Substitutions, and More...

Not feeling spicy? Use mild Italian sausage, bratwurst, or kielbasa. Either purple cabbage or green cabbage can be used, based on preference. For a smoky kick, swap smoked paprika for sweet paprika. Garnish with fresh chopped parsley.

PER SERVING
Calories: 562 | Fat: 30g | Protein: 43g | Sodium: 2,127mg | Fiber: 2g | Carbohydrates: 30g | Sugar: 3g

CHAPTER SEVEN

FAMILY GRILL NIGHTS

Often when you see dinner recipes for the grill, the recipe only focuses on the protein, such as a grilled chicken recipe with a special marinade, or a grilled fish. But what about the side dishes? Just grilling protein means there is still a lot of cooking to do somewhere else.

The following chapter solves this problem with a creative selection of complete dinner recipes made entirely on the grill. Whether you are a year-round or seasonal griller, the easy recipes in this chapter will quickly become family favorites. You will find familiar dishes like Barbecue Chicken Thighs with Corn on the Cob and Arugula Salad with easy shortcuts and less prep work. Learn how to make Grilled Flank Steak with Summer Squash and Pesto Toast in under 30 minutes, as well as the easiest-ever Taco Salmon with Avocado Lime Mash and Grilled Tomatoes.

Taco Salmon with Avocado Lime Mash and Grilled Tomatoes

SERVES 4

Create a tasty dinner in minutes by seasoning salmon fillets with taco seasoning, grilling halved vine-on tomatoes, and making an Avocado Lime Mash right on the cutting board—no need for extra dishes!

PREP TIME: 8 MINUTES • ACTIVE COOK TIME: 8 MINUTES • HANDS-OFF COOK TIME: N/A

For Salmon

4 (6-ounce, ½"-thick) wild Alaskan salmon fillets, patted dry

2 tablespoons avocado oil

4 tablespoons taco seasoning

4 vine-on tomatoes, halved

Avocado oil cooking spray

¼ teaspoon kosher salt

¼ teaspoon ground black pepper

1 medium lime, quartered

1. To make Salmon: With lid closed, preheat gas grill for 10 minutes for two-zone cooking, with one side set to high heat and one side set to medium-low.

2. Rub ½ tablespoon avocado oil on both sides of each salmon piece. Finish with 1 tablespoon taco seasoning per piece.

3. Spray each tomato half with avocado oil spray and sprinkle all halves with salt and pepper.

4. Open lid, lightly oil grill grates with high-heat cooking oil such as avocado oil, and place salmon skin side down on high-heat side. Place tomatoes cut side down on medium-low side. Close lid and cook 4 minutes.

5. Open lid, then use a fish turner or sturdy flipper to flip salmon and transfer to medium-low side. Flip tomatoes so that the cut side is up. Close lid and grill 2–3 more minutes until salmon has reached internal temperature of 140°F and flakes easily with a fork.

Continued ▶

For Avocado Lime Mash

2 large avocados, peeled and pitted

Juice of 1 medium lime

1/2 teaspoon kosher salt

6 To make Avocado Lime Mash: On a cutting board, mash avocados with lime juice and salt. Divide among four plates.

7 Open lid, remove salmon and tomatoes from grill, and transfer one piece of salmon and two tomato halves to each plate with Avocado Lime Mash. Serve immediately with a quarter of lime on the side.

PER SERVING
Calories: 376 | Fat: 21g | Protein: 38g | Sodium: 655mg | Fiber: 3g | Carbohydrates: 9g | Sugar: 3g

Tips, Substitutions, and More...

Cooking times for salmon will change based on thickness. To add a kick of heat, add 1/8 teaspoon cayenne pepper to the taco seasoning before rubbing onto the salmon.

Creole Shrimp, Zucchini, and Peppers

SERVES 4

It's hard to believe that this flavorful dish is only made with five simple ingredients, but it's a magical combination! Take care to layer the ingredients as listed to get the best results and don't skip the resting step: This is for the shrimp to finish cooking.

PREP TIME: 10 MINUTES • ACTIVE COOK TIME: N/A • HANDS-OFF COOK TIME: 20 MINUTES

1 pound zucchini, ends trimmed, quartered, and cut into $1/2$" pieces

$1^1/2$ pounds uncooked, shell-on large shrimp, fresh or defrosted and drained

2 tablespoons creole seasoning

8 tablespoons salted butter

1 (1-pound) bag frozen mixed bell pepper strips

1 With lid closed, preheat gas grill to medium-high heat for 10 minutes. Spray center of four 12" × 24" sheets of aluminum foil with nonstick cooking spray.

2 In center of each foil, arrange $1/4$ zucchini pieces, $1/4$ shrimp, $1^1/2$ teaspoons creole seasoning, 2 tablespoons butter, and $1/4$ pepper strips. Bring short sides of foil together, fold down to make a seam, and crimp to seal tightly. Crimp remaining open ends of packets, leaving as much headroom as possible inside packets for steaming process.

3 Open lid and place packets directly on grill grates, then close lid and cook undisturbed 10 minutes.

4 Open lid, remove packets from grill, and allow to rest 10 minutes (to steam more) before opening. Mix ingredients to distribute creole butter and serve immediately.

Tips, Substitutions, and More...

Shrimp in the shell work beautifully for this recipe, as the shrimp stay very moist and tender. However, if you don't want to deal with peeling the shells on your dinner plate, look for already peeled and deveined shrimp at the grocery store. This dish is excellent served over reheated rice for a heartier meal.

PER SERVING
Calories: 321 | Fat: 23g | Protein: 24g | Sodium: 1,063mg | Fiber: 1g | Carbohydrates: 4g | Sugar: 3g

Barbecue Chicken Thighs with Corn on the Cob and Arugula Salad

SERVES 4

This simplified version of a summer classic pairs quick-cooking chicken thighs with whole corn on the cob and arugula salad for a memorable meal. Simply grill chicken and baste with barbecue sauce just a few minutes before the end of the cooking time to ensure that the barbecue sauce caramelizes.

PREP TIME: 10 MINUTES • ACTIVE COOK TIME: 15 MINUTES • HANDS-OFF COOK TIME: N/A

4 medium ears corn on the cob, husks and silk removed

Nonstick avocado cooking spray

4 (6-ounce) boneless, skinless chicken thighs

1 teaspoon kosher salt

1/2 cup Kansas City–style barbecue sauce

2 cups baby arugula

4 teaspoons extra-virgin olive oil

2 teaspoons balsamic vinegar

Tips, Substitutions, and More...

Save even more time by buying a package of corn that already has the husks removed. Note that very large or thick chicken thighs can take longer to cook. Chicken should be cooked to an internal temperature of 165°F at the thickest part. Both the chicken and corn can be made ahead of time and served chilled.

1 With lid closed, preheat gas grill to medium-high heat for 10 minutes.

2 Spray corn with nonstick cooking spray and set on a baking sheet or tray. Add chicken thighs to sheet or tray. Spray both sides with nonstick cooking spray and sprinkle salt all over chicken pieces.

3 Open lid, lightly oil grill grates with high-heat cooking oil such as avocado oil, and place chicken thighs and corn on grill. Cook, lid up, 5 minutes. Do not turn chicken yet but rotate the corn at least once.

4 Flip each chicken thigh, rotate corn again, close lid, and cook 4 minutes.

5 Open lid, rotate corn, and baste half of barbecue sauce on chicken. Flip chicken and baste the other side with remaining barbecue sauce. Keeping lid open, cook 2 minutes, then rotate corn again and flip chicken one more time. Cook 2 more minutes.

6 Remove chicken and corn to four dinner plates. Divide arugula onto plates and drizzle arugula on each plate with 1 teaspoon olive oil and 1/2 teaspoon balsamic vinegar. Serve.

PER SERVING
Calories: 499 | Fat: 22g | Protein: 39g | Sodium: 803mg | Fiber: 3g | Carbohydrates: 36g | Sugar: 16g

Adobo Swordfish with Pico de Gallo and Broccolini

SERVES
4

A complete dinner that is on the table in about 15 minutes start to finish. Make sure to look for ½"-thick swordfish steaks. If the steaks are thicker, you will have to increase the cooking time. Serve alongside quickly grilled broccolini and tortilla chips. To mix it up, try plantain chips or cassava chips.

PREP TIME: 5 MINUTES ● ACTIVE COOK TIME: 8 MINUTES ● HANDS-OFF COOK TIME: N/A

4 (6-ounce, ½"-thick) swordfish steaks, patted dry

4 tablespoons avocado oil, divided

4 tablespoons adobo seasoning

1 pound broccolini

½ teaspoon kosher salt

¼ teaspoon ground black pepper

½ cup pico de gallo

4 ounces corn tortilla chips

1 With lid closed, preheat gas grill to medium heat for 10 minutes. While grill is preheating, place swordfish on a cutting board and rub both sides of each steak with ½ tablespoon oil and 1 tablespoon adobo seasoning.

2 On a cutting board, toss broccolini with remaining 2 tablespoons oil, salt, and pepper.

3 Open lid, lightly oil grill grates with high-heat cooking oil such as avocado oil, and place seasoned swordfish steaks on grill. Close lid and cook undisturbed 3½ minutes.

4 Open lid, flip swordfish, and add broccolini. Keeping lid open, cook both for 4 minutes, flipping broccolini every 45 seconds.

5 Serve swordfish topped with pico de gallo, alongside cooked broccolini and tortilla chips.

PER SERVING
Calories: 592 | Fat: 37g | Protein: 40g | Sodium: 3,307mg | Fiber: 5g | Carbohydrates: 25g | Sugar: 0g

Tandoori-Spiced Pork Tenderloin with Asparagus and Naan

SERVES 4

This Tandoori-Spiced Pork Tenderloin with Asparagus and Naan is a quick and flavorful dish that brings the vibrant tastes of Indian cuisine to your table. Served with a zesty Yogurt Sauce, the pork tenderloin is coated in tandoori seasoning and grilled to perfection alongside asparagus, then paired with warmed naan bread and sliced cucumbers.

PREP TIME: 10 MINUTES • ACTIVE COOK TIME: 20 MINUTES
HANDS-OFF COOK TIME: 10 MINUTES RESTING TIME

For Yogurt Sauce

1 cup full-fat plain yogurt

Juice of 1 medium lemon

$1/2$ teaspoon kosher salt

$1/4$ cup finely chopped fresh cilantro leaves

2 cloves garlic, peeled and crushed

1 With lid closed, preheat gas grill for 10 minutes for two-zone cooking, with $2/3$ of the burners set to high heat and $1/3$ of the burners set to medium-low.

2 To make Yogurt Sauce: In a small bowl, combine ingredients and set aside.

For Pork and Sides

1 (1$1/2$-pound) pork tenderloin, trimmed and patted dry

1 tablespoon extra-virgin olive oil

2 tablespoons tandoori seasoning

1 pound asparagus, ends trimmed by 1"

Avocado oil cooking spray

$1/4$ teaspoon kosher salt

$1/8$ teaspoon ground black pepper

4 fresh or frozen naan breads

2 medium English cucumbers, sliced

3 To make Pork and Sides: Rub all sides of pork tenderloin with oil and tandoori seasoning. Spray asparagus with avocado oil spray and sprinkle with salt and pepper.

Continued ▶

4 Open lid and lightly oil grill grates with high-heat cooking oil such as avocado oil, add pork to the high-heat side of grill, and grill each of the two largest sides 2½ minutes (for a total of 5 minutes), keeping lid closed between flipping.

5 Transfer pork to medium-low side of grill and grill each of the two largest sides 5 minutes each (for a total of 10 minutes), keeping lid closed between flipping.

6 Open lid. Remove pork to a serving plate or cutting board and allow to rest 10 minutes before slicing into ¼" slices.

7 While pork is resting, add asparagus directly to grates of high-heat side of grill and grill 4–5 minutes, flipping at least twice during cooking time, until asparagus are beginning to char but are not burning. Keep lid closed in between flipping.

8 Add naan to top rack of grill to reheat through while asparagus is cooking. Check frequently to avoid burning.

9 Serve pork tenderloin with Yogurt Sauce, grilled asparagus, sliced cucumber, and naan on the side.

PER SERVING
Calories: 569 | Fat: 15g | Protein: 51g | Sodium: 896mg | Fiber: 5g | Carbohydrates: 57g | Sugar: 10g

Tips, Substitutions, and More...

If tandoori seasoning is salt-free, add 1½ teaspoons kosher salt. If you don't have regular yogurt, substitute full-fat Greek yogurt and thin it out with some whole milk. Don't skip resting the pork tenderloin: It's necessary to ensure it's the proper temperature in the center before you slice it.

Barbecue Cheddar Burgers with Quick Pickled Onions

SERVES 4

Quick pickling red onions elevates this familiar burger combination and balances the sweetness of the barbecue sauce. Thick slices of Cheddar cheese and crispy shredded iceberg lettuce put the finishing touches on a simple dinner that tastes fancy. Serve with sliced cucumber and your favorite potato chips.

PREP TIME: 10 MINUTES • ACTIVE COOK TIME: 8 MINUTES • HANDS-OFF COOK TIME: N/A

For Quick Pickled Onions

1 medium red onion, peeled, halved, and thinly sliced

3/4 cup apple cider vinegar

1/4 cup water

1/2 teaspoon kosher salt

1 teaspoon granulated sugar

1 With lid closed, preheat gas grill to medium-high heat for 10 minutes.

2 To make Quick Pickled Onions: In a glass jar or container with a lid, combine onion with vinegar, water, salt, and sugar. Place lid on and set aside.

For Burgers

4 (1/4-pound, 1/4"-thick) beef burger patties

4 (1-ounce) slices Cheddar cheese

4 seeded burger buns

4 tablespoons Kansas City–style barbecue sauce

1 (8-ounce) bag shredded iceberg lettuce

3 To make Burgers: Open grill lid and lightly oil grill grates with high-heat cooking oil such as avocado oil. Add burger patties, close lid, and cook undisturbed 3 minutes.

4 Open lid, flip burgers, close lid, and cook 3 more minutes.

Continued ▶

5 Open lid, place a slice of cheese on each burger. Set burger buns, cut side down, on upper rack. Close lid 45 seconds or until buns are lightly toasted and cheese is melted.

6 Open lid. Remove buns and cheeseburgers from grill and turn off. Add 1 tablespoon barbecue sauce to the bottom of each bun. Top with Quick Pickled Onions, cheeseburger, lettuce, and bun top. Serve immediately.

PER SERVING
Calories: 417 | Fat: 18g | Protein: 34g | Sodium: 520mg | Fiber: 2g | Carbohydrates: 30g | Sugar: 11g

Tips, Substitutions, and More...

Save time by buying premade burger patties. Just place them between two layers of parchment and flatten slightly if they are super thick. If the burgers are thicker, adjust the cooking time before adding the cheese. Burgers should be cooked until an internal temperature of 160°F is reached.

Chicken, Tomato, and Fennel Foil Packets

SERVES 4

The polenta rounds provide the perfect base for the seasoned chicken and ensure that it doesn't dry out. The juice from the fresh-cut fennel and tomatoes mixes with the butter and spices to create a delicious sauce. A grilling recipe with totally hands-off cooking time to allow for more socializing time with family and friends!

PREP TIME: 15 MINUTES • ACTIVE COOK TIME: N/A • HANDS-OFF COOK TIME: 29 MINUTES

1 (18-ounce) tube prepared polenta, cut into 12 slices

4 (6-ounce) skinless, boneless chicken breasts

1 teaspoon dried parsley

1 teaspoon kosher salt

1/2 teaspoon ground black pepper

1/2 teaspoon dried thyme

1/4 teaspoon crushed red pepper flakes

1 fennel bulb, stalks discarded, bulb quartered and cut into 1/2" slices, layers separated

4 vine-on tomatoes, quartered

4 tablespoons salted butter

1 With lid closed, preheat gas grill to medium-high heat for 10 minutes. Cut four 12" × 20" pieces of aluminum foil. Place all four on a work surface and spray each with nonstick cooking spray.

2 Place 3 slices polenta in center of each piece of foil. Top each with 1 chicken breast. Evenly divide parsley, salt, black pepper, thyme, and red pepper flakes over chicken.

3 Divide fennel and tomatoes on top of chicken. Top each with 1 tablespoon butter. Close up packets by folding short sides up to each other, taking care to leave some headroom of air at top. Fold down to make a seam and crimp seam. Twist ends and fold up to make two "handles."

4 Once grill is preheated, open lid and carefully place each packet directly on grill grates, then close lid and cook undisturbed 22–24 minutes (depending on thickness of chicken) until internal temperature of 165°F is reached.

5 Open lid. Remove packets from grill and allow to rest 5 minutes (to steam more) before opening. Carefully open each packet and slide ingredients onto dinner plates. Serve.

PER SERVING
Calories: 515 | Fat: 18g | Protein: 56g | Sodium: 1,054mg | Fiber: 4g | Carbohydrates: 30g | Sugar: 5g

Grilled Flank Steak with Summer Squash and Pesto Toast

SERVES 4

This Grilled Flank Steak with Summer Squash and Pesto Toast is a delightful ensemble of flavors and textures that captures the essence of summer on your plate. With a quick 10-minute prep time and 16 minutes of active cook time, it's a perfect choice for a hassle-free yet gourmet meal.

PREP TIME: 10 MINUTES • ACTIVE COOK TIME: 16 MINUTES • HANDS-OFF COOK TIME: N/A

4 tablespoons basil pesto

1 (6-ounce) white baguette, cut into 4 sections

2 pounds flank steak, about 1/2" thick

1 pound yellow summer squash, ends trimmed, quartered lengthwise

1 tablespoon avocado oil

2 teaspoons kosher salt

1 teaspoon ground black pepper

1 With lid closed, preheat gas grill for 10 minutes for two-zone cooking, with one side set to high heat and one side set to medium.

2 Spread 1 tablespoon pesto over each section of baguette (sliced side) and set aside.

3 Place flank steak and squash on a baking sheet. Divide oil, salt, and pepper over steak and squash until all pieces are coated.

4 Open lid, lightly oil grill grates with high-heat cooking oil such as avocado oil, and add flank steak to the high-heat side. Close lid and cook 4 minutes, opening lid to flip steak once during cooking time.

5 Open lid, move steak to medium-heat side, and cook 4 more minutes, opening lid to flip steak once during cooking time.

Continued ▶

6 Open lid. Remove steak from grill and set aside to rest. Turn all grill knobs to medium heat, add squash, and close lid. Keeping lid closed, cook 7–8 minutes until squash begins to char but is not burned, flipping each piece twice during cooking time.

7 Add pesto bread (pesto side up) for the last 2 minutes of cooking time (on the elevated rack if you have one).

8 Remove squash and bread, slice steak against the grain, and serve immediately.

PER SERVING
Calories: 557 | Fat: 23g | Protein: 54g | Sodium: 1,402mg | Fiber: 4g | Carbohydrates: 34g | Sugar: 0g

Tips, Substitutions, and More...

Zucchini can be substituted but increase the grilling time by 90 seconds or 2 minutes. If your grill doesn't have an elevated cooking rack, watch the bread carefully so the bottom doesn't burn. It may only need 60–90 seconds on the main grill grates. For an extra-cheesy bread, add 1 tablespoon shredded mozzarella or Parmesan to each pesto toast after adding the pesto.

CHAPTER EIGHT

INSTANT DINNERS

The Instant Pot® is a lifesaver when you are short on time and want to reduce effort. Meals that would typically take hours can be prepared in a fraction of the cooking time, mostly hands-off. Additionally, the versatility of the Instant Pot® functionality allows for sautéing before cooking to build layers of flavor.

In this chapter, you will find out how to create flavorfully complex yet easy dinners such as Jalapeño Popper Mac 'n' Cheese in minutes, make better-than-takeout Black Bean and Chicken Burrito Bowls, and learn how to make a Vegetarian Risotto with Parmesan without any hands-on stirring! You will also learn the secret to making a perfect meat-loaded pasta dinner with no straining or extra pots—and more!

Vegetarian Risotto with Parmesan

SERVES
6

The Instant Pot® is a risotto magician, allowing you to create a creamy, delicious, and perfectly tender risotto without any obsessive stirring and adding additional broth during cooking. This vegetarian version is loaded with sautéed mushrooms, sun-dried tomatoes, peas, and Parmesan. Make sure to pull the peas out of the freezer at the very start of the recipe: They will be stirred into the hot risotto when it's done cooking and need to be thawed to heat through!

PREP TIME: 8 MINUTES ● ACTIVE COOK TIME: 5 MINUTES ● HANDS-OFF COOK TIME: 16 MINUTES (10 MINUTES TO PRESSURE + 6 MINUTES COOKING TIME)

6 tablespoons salted butter, divided

1 medium yellow onion, peeled, quartered, and thinly sliced

1 (10-ounce) package sliced white mushrooms

6 cloves garlic, peeled and crushed

1/2 cup loosely packed sun-dried tomatoes, sliced into thin strips on short side

1 teaspoon kosher salt

1/2 teaspoon ground black pepper

1/2 teaspoon dried thyme

1/4 teaspoon crushed red pepper flakes

3/4 cup dry white wine

4 cups low-sodium vegetable broth

2 cups arborio rice, unrinsed

1 cup frozen peas, thawed

1/2 cup grated Parmesan cheese

1 Place the insert in the 6-quart Instant Pot®. Press the Sauté button and select High/More.

2 Add 4 tablespoons butter to pot. As soon as butter is melted, add onion, mushrooms, garlic, sun-dried tomatoes, and spices. Sauté 4 minutes, stirring frequently, or until mushrooms and onions begin to soften.

3 Add wine to pot and cook 1 minute, using a spatula to scrape the bottom of insert, then press Cancel to turn off Instant Pot®.

4 Add broth and rice, then stir to combine. Close lid, press the Manual or Pressure Cook button, and set time to 6 minutes at High Pressure. When the timer beeps, immediately quick-release the pressure until the float valve drops. Press the Cancel button and open lid.

5 Stir in thawed peas and remaining 2 tablespoons butter until butter is melted. Add Parmesan. Stir to combine and serve immediately.

PER SERVING
Calories: 388 | Fat: 13g | Protein: 10g | Sodium: 682mg | Fiber: 2g | Carbohydrates: 57g | Sugar: 5g

Creamy Chicken Soup with Gnocchi and Kale

SERVES 6

This Creamy Chicken Soup combines the convenience of a bag of cleaned and chopped kale with already shredded rotisserie chicken and quick-cooking potato gnocchi to deliver a bowl of hearty dinner goodness. Excellent served with crushed red pepper flakes, a touch of extra grated Parmesan, and freshly chopped parsley on top.

PREP TIME: 5 MINUTES • ACTIVE COOK TIME: 5 MINUTES
HANDS-OFF COOK TIME: 20 MINUTES (15 MINUTES TO PRESSURE + 5 MINUTES WARMING TIME)

2 tablespoons extra-virgin olive oil

1 medium yellow onion, peeled, halved, and thinly sliced

2 medium stalks celery, diced

4 cloves garlic, peeled and crushed

2 teaspoons Italian seasoning

1 teaspoon kosher salt

1/2 teaspoon ground black pepper

1/2 teaspoon dried thyme

1/2 teaspoon ground turmeric

6 cups low-sodium chicken broth

12 ounces shredded rotisserie chicken

8 ounces cleaned and chopped fresh kale

1 pound shelf-stable vacuum-packed potato gnocchi

1 cup half-and-half

1/2 cup grated Parmesan cheese

1. Place the insert in the 6-quart Instant Pot®. Press the Sauté button and select Medium/Normal. Once hot, add oil and then onion, celery, garlic, and spices. Sauté 5 minutes, stirring occasionally, or until vegetables begin to soften.

2. Press Cancel to turn off Instant Pot®. Add broth, chicken, and kale. Stir to combine. Close lid, press the Manual or Pressure Cook button, and set time to 0 minutes at High Pressure. When the timer beeps (after about 15 minutes), quick-release the pressure until the float valve drops. Press the Cancel button and open lid.

3. Immediately stir in gnocchi and allow to sit undisturbed 5 minutes to warm the gnocchi.

4. Stir in half-and-half and Parmesan and serve.

PER SERVING
Calories: 428 | Fat: 20g | Protein: 23g | Sodium: 1,207mg | Fiber: 2g | Carbohydrates: 39g | Sugar: 3g

Chicken and Spinach Curry in a Hurry

SERVES 4

This ridiculously easy Chicken and Spinach Curry in a Hurry tastes amazing and takes very little effort to pull together. Just add all of the ingredients (except for the spinach) in the Instant Pot®, let it work its magic, stir in the spinach, and voilà: Dinner is served.

PREP TIME: 5 MINUTES • ACTIVE COOK TIME: N/A
HANDS-OFF COOK TIME: 17 MINUTES (12 MINUTES TO PRESSURE + 5 MINUTES COOKING TIME)

1 (14-ounce) can full-fat coconut milk

2 tablespoons tomato paste

1 tablespoon curry powder

1 teaspoon kosher salt

1/2 teaspoon ground ginger

1/4 teaspoon ground black pepper

1/4 teaspoon cayenne pepper

6 cloves garlic, peeled and crushed

1 1/2 pounds boneless, skinless chicken thighs

1 (5-ounce) bag fresh baby spinach

3 cups reheated precooked white rice

1 Place the insert in the 6-quart Instant Pot®. Combine coconut milk, tomato paste, spices, and garlic in the pot. Add chicken.

2 Close lid, press the Manual or Pressure Cook button, and set time to 5 minutes at High Pressure. When the timer beeps, immediately quick-release the pressure until the float valve drops. Press the Cancel button and open lid.

3 Keeping cooked chicken in the Instant Pot®, use two forks to quickly pull apart chicken and shred. Stir in spinach until wilted. Serve alongside rice.

PER SERVING
Calories: 805 | Fat: 33g | Protein: 40g | Sodium: 673mg | Fiber: 3g | Carbohydrates: 87g | Sugar: 5g

Tips, Substitutions, and More...

This curry is mild. To add some heat, add chopped serrano or jalapeño pepper or increase the cayenne pepper to 1 teaspoon. Not in the mood for rice? Substitute warmed naan bread instead!

Smoky Chicken and Wild Rice Soup

Wild rice is notorious for taking a long time to cook. The Instant Pot® makes quick work of this whole grain. The pressurized environment leaves a perfectly tender and appropriately chewy split rice grain that adds so much texture and flavor to this thick and hearty dinner soup.

**PREP TIME: 10 MINUTES • ACTIVE COOK TIME: 5 MINUTES
HANDS-OFF COOK TIME: 60 MINUTES (20 MINUTES TO PRESSURE +
20 MINUTES COOKING TIME + 20 MINUTES NATURAL PRESSURE RELEASE)**

2 tablespoons extra-virgin olive oil

1 large yellow onion, peeled and chopped

4 medium stalks celery, cut into 1/8" half-moons

4 cloves garlic, peeled and crushed

1 (10-ounce) package sliced white mushrooms

2 1/2 teaspoons kosher salt

2 teaspoons dried parsley

1 teaspoon smoked paprika

1 teaspoon dried thyme

1/2 teaspoon ground cumin

1/2 teaspoon ground black pepper

1 1/2 cups black wild rice, rinsed

8 cups low-sodium chicken broth

1 pound boneless, skinless chicken breast

2 cups frozen crinkle cut carrot rounds

2 tablespoons finely chopped fresh parsley

1 Place the insert in the 6-quart Instant Pot®. Press the Sauté button and select High/More. Once hot, add oil, then onion, celery, garlic, mushrooms, and spices. Sauté 4 minutes, stirring frequently. Press Cancel to turn off Instant Pot®.

2 Add rice and broth, and stir to combine.

3 Submerge chicken into broth mixture, taking care to keep rice grains submerged.

4 Close lid, press the Manual or Pressure Cook button, and set time to 20 minutes at High Pressure.

5 When the timer beeps, let pressure release naturally for 20 minutes, then quick-release remaining steam.

6 Press the Cancel button, open lid, and transfer chicken to a cutting board. Immediately stir carrots into pot and place lid back on (doesn't have to be locked, just resting on top to keep heat in).

7 Use two forks to shred chicken and transfer back to soup. Top with chopped parsley. Serve.

PER SERVING
Calories: 194 | Fat: 6g | Protein: 21g | Sodium: 740mg | Fiber: 2g | Carbohydrates: 14g | Sugar: 3g

Black Bean and Chicken Burrito Bowls

SERVES 4

Skip expensive takeout and make these Black Bean and Chicken Burrito Bowls with just 10 minutes of prep work. The trick to this recipe is layering the ingredients in the order listed and resisting the urge to stir! Then, serve with a medley of your favorite toppings, such as sour cream, and some tortilla chips if you have them on hand.

PREP TIME: 10 MINUTES • ACTIVE COOK TIME: N/A
HANDS-OFF COOK TIME: 25 MINUTES (15 MINUTES TO PRESSURE + 10 MINUTES COOKING TIME)

2 tablespoons avocado oil

1 pound boneless, skinless chicken breast, cut into 1" chunks

3 tablespoons plus 1 teaspoon taco seasoning

1 cup low-sodium chicken broth

1 cup jasmine rice, rinsed

1 (15-ounce) can black beans, drained and rinsed

1 cup frozen sweet corn kernels

1 (4-ounce) can diced green chiles

1 cup chunky salsa

Tips, Substitutions, and More…

To add a kick of heat, swap spicy salsa for mild. Substitute canned pinto or kidney beans for black beans if preferred. Cubed boneless, skinless chicken thighs can substitute for chicken breast. Serve with your favorite toppings! Try a Mexican cheese blend, diced avocado or guacamole, sour cream, pickled jalapeños, and finely chopped cilantro leaves and scallions.

1 Place the insert in the 6-quart Instant Pot®. Add ingredients in order listed. Do not stir between each layer. Use a spoon to spread out each layer evenly. If necessary, use a spoon to push the rice layer down under broth before moving on to black bean layer.

2 Close lid, press the Manual or Pressure Cook button, and set time to 10 minutes at High Pressure. When the timer beeps, immediately quick-pressure the release until the float valve drops. Press the Cancel button and open lid.

3 Use a fork to gently fluff rice, divide mixture into four bowls, and serve with your favorite toppings.

PER SERVING
Calories: 563 | Fat: 12g | Protein: 38g |
Sodium: 1,250mg | Fiber: 9g | Carbohydrates: 76g |
Sugar: 7g

Dump and Go Pasta Dinner

SERVES 4

This Dump and Go Pasta Dinner is truly the quickest, most hands-off way to make a delicious pasta dinner. There is no prep work—just open the packages, dump, and let the Instant Pot® do the rest. No draining pasta, no separate pot for sauce. Excellent served topped with crushed red pepper flakes and grated Parmesan! Substitute mild or hot uncooked bulk Italian sausage for ground beef if preferred.

PREP TIME: N/A ● ACTIVE COOK TIME: 6 MINUTES ● HANDS-OFF COOK TIME: 22 MINUTES (15 MINUTES TO PRESSURE + 5 MINUTES COOKING TIME + 2 MINUTES NATURAL PRESSURE RELEASE)

2 tablespoons extra-virgin olive oil

1 pound 80% lean ground beef

1 pound uncooked bow tie pasta

5 cups water

1 (24-ounce) jar marinara sauce

1 (5-ounce) bag fresh baby spinach

Tips, Substitutions, and More...

This recipe is best with short, sturdy pasta shapes such as bow ties, fusilli, penne, ziti, etc. To substitute other shapes for the bow ties, check the package cooking time, round down to an even number, cut the number in half, and add 1 minute. For example: Penne pasta takes 13 minutes to cook; round down to 12 minutes, divide in half to 6, and add 1 minute for 7 minutes in Instant Pot®.

1 Place the insert in the 6-quart Instant Pot®. Press the Sauté button and select High/More. Once hot, add oil and ground beef. Sauté 5 minutes, stirring frequently, or until beef is broken up in chunks and mostly brown. Press Cancel to turn off Instant Pot®.

2 Add pasta on top of meat; do not stir. Add water, do not stir, and use a spoon to push down pasta under the water as much as possible. It's okay if some is sticking out as sauce will cover it. Add marinara sauce; do not stir.

3 Close lid, press the Manual or Pressure Cook button, and set time to 5 minutes at High Pressure. When the timer beeps, let pressure release naturally for 2 minutes, then quick-release remaining steam.

4 Press the Cancel button, open lid, and stir in spinach until wilted, about 1 minute. Serve.

PER SERVING
Calories: 609 | Fat: 33g | Protein: 29g | Sodium: 817mg | Fiber: 4g | Carbohydrates: 50g | Sugar: 10g

Jalapeño Popper Mac 'n' Cheese

SERVES
6

Jalapeño Popper Mac 'n' Cheese captures the beloved flavor of the popular appetizer, but simplifies it by using already diced pancetta in place of bacon and tangy pickled jalapeños from a jar to save time from chopping and prepping fresh jalapeños. The Instant Pot® perfectly cooks the pasta without the need to strain and eliminates a second pot.

PREP TIME: 5 MINUTES ● ACTIVE COOK TIME: 10 MINUTES
HANDS-OFF COOK TIME: 15 MINUTES (10 MINUTES TO PRESSURE + 5 MINUTES COOKING TIME)

4 tablespoons salted butter, divided

8 ounces diced pancetta

1 pound uncooked elbow macaroni pasta

4 cups low-sodium chicken broth

1 teaspoon Frank's RedHot Original Cayenne Pepper Sauce

1 teaspoon garlic powder

1/2 teaspoon kosher salt

8 ounces shredded Cheddar cheese

8 ounces shredded Monterey jack cheese

3/4 cup whole milk

1/2 cup sliced pickled jalapeños, drained and roughly chopped

1 Place the insert in the 6-quart Instant Pot®. Press the Sauté button and select High/More.

2 Add 2 tablespoons butter and pancetta to pot. Sauté 8 minutes, stirring occasionally, or until pancetta begins to brown. Remove pancetta to a medium bowl; drain off excess fat and discard. Press Cancel to turn off Instant Pot®.

3 Add pasta, broth, hot sauce, garlic, and salt to pot. Use a spatula to scrape bottom of pot, stir, and make sure that all pasta is fully submerged under broth.

4 Close lid, press the Manual or Pressure Cook button, and set time to 5 minutes at High Pressure. When the timer beeps, immediately quick-release the pressure until the float valve drops. Press the Cancel button and open lid.

5 Stir in remaining butter and both cheeses in batches until fully melted, about 90 seconds. Add milk, jalapeños, and cooked pancetta to the pasta and cheese mixture. Stir until mixed well (about 30 seconds) and serve immediately.

PER SERVING
Calories: 698 | Fat: 38g | Protein: 30g | Sodium: 680mg | Fiber: 3g | Carbohydrates: 60g | Sugar: 4g

Lamb Korma with Potatoes and Peas

SERVES
4

The beauty of lamb stew meat is that once it is cooked properly, it's tender and succulent and falls apart like butter. The tricky part is getting there. The Instant Pot® tenderizes the tough lamb meat in no time, making this dish hassle-free. It's excellent served with either reheated rice or warmed naan bread on the side and topped with chopped cilantro.

PREP TIME: 5 MINUTES ● ACTIVE COOK TIME: 6 MINUTES ● HANDS-OFF COOK TIME: 40 MINUTES (10 MINUTES TO PRESSURE + 15 MINUTES COOKING TIME + 15 MINUTES NATURAL PRESSURE RELEASE)

2 tablespoons avocado oil

1$\frac{1}{2}$ pounds lamb stew meat, cut into 1" cubes

1 medium yellow onion, peeled, halved, and thinly sliced

2 tablespoons yellow curry paste

1 (15-ounce) can full-fat coconut milk

1 pound pearl potatoes

2 cups frozen peas

1 Place the insert in the 6-quart Instant Pot®. Press the Sauté button and select High/More. Add oil. Once hot, add lamb and onion. Sauté 5 minutes, stirring occasionally, or until onions soften and meat begins to brown.

2 Press Cancel to turn off Instant Pot®. Add curry paste and stir until dissolved, about 30 seconds. Add coconut milk and potatoes. Close lid, press the Manual or Pressure Cook button, and set time to 15 minutes at High Pressure.

3 When the timer beeps, let pressure release naturally for 15 minutes, then quick-release remaining steam. Press the Cancel button and open lid. Immediately stir in peas to warm through. Serve.

Tips, Substitutions, and More...

To save even more time, use a 15-ounce jar of korma curry simmer sauce (like Patak's) in place of the canned coconut milk and curry paste. Alternatively, substitute massaman curry paste for yellow. If you can't find pearl potatoes, use quartered, unpeeled Yukon Gold potatoes.

PER SERVING
Calories: 729 | Fat: 46g | Protein: 40g | Sodium: 685mg | Fiber: 2g | Carbohydrates: 40g | Sugar: 7g

Pork Stew with Potatoes, Peppers, and Onions

This flavorful Pork Stew with Potatoes, Peppers, and Onions is a hearty one pot dinner loaded with texture and savory ingredients. The pressure environment of the Instant Pot® delivers succulent pork stew meat paired with perfectly tender vegetables in a rich broth. Serve with crusty bread and butter or alongside reheated rice or mashed potatoes.

**PREP TIME: 10 MINUTES • ACTIVE COOK TIME: 10 MINUTES
HANDS-OFF COOK TIME: 45 MINUTES (15 MINUTES TO PRESSURE +
20 MINUTES COOKING TIME + 10 MINUTES NATURAL PRESSURE RELEASE)**

2 tablespoons extra-virgin olive oil

3 pounds pork stew meat, cut into 1" cubes

1 medium yellow onion, peeled, halved, and thinly sliced

2 teaspoons kosher salt

1 tablespoon dried oregano

$1/2$ teaspoon ground black pepper

$1/2$ teaspoon fennel seeds

$1/4$ teaspoon crushed red pepper flakes

$3/4$ cup low-sodium chicken broth

1 (15-ounce) can diced no-salt tomatoes

6 cloves garlic, peeled and crushed

2 pounds Yukon Gold potatoes, unpeeled, cut into 1" chunks

1 (1-pound) bag frozen mixed bell pepper strips

1 (5-ounce) bag fresh baby spinach

Juice of 1 medium lemon

1 Place the insert in the 6-quart Instant Pot®. Press the Sauté button and select High/More.

2 Once hot, add oil and some pork (enough for a non-crowded single layer on the bottom of Instant Pot® insert), along with onion and spices. Cook undisturbed 4 minutes, flip, and cook an additional 4 minutes.

3 Press Cancel to turn off Instant Pot®. Add broth, tomatoes, garlic, potatoes, remaining pork, and bell pepper; stir to combine.

4 Close lid, press the Manual or Pressure Cook button, and set time to 20 minutes at High Pressure. When the timer beeps, let pressure release naturally for 10 minutes, then quick-release remaining steam. Press the Cancel button and open lid.

5 Stir in spinach until wilted, about 90 seconds. Stir in lemon juice and serve.

PER SERVING
Calories: 366 | Fat: 10g | Protein: 23g | Sodium: 777mg | Fiber: 7g | Carbohydrates: 46g | Sugar: 11g

Cheesy Chili Mac with Beans

SERVES 6

Cheesy Chili Mac with Beans combines the familiar flavors of your favorite beef and bean chili with the indulgent goodness of mac 'n' cheese. This comforting one pot dinner recipe features ground beef, kidney beans, elbow macaroni, tomatoes, corn, and the perfect blend of spices, along with gooey melted cheese, to create a satisfying dinner that needs minimal cleanup!

PREP TIME: 5 MINUTES • ACTIVE COOK TIME: 5 MINUTES
HANDS-OFF COOK TIME: 17 MINUTES (12 MINUTES TO PRESSURE + 5 MINUTES COOKING TIME)

2 tablespoons avocado oil

1½ pounds 80% lean ground beef

1 medium yellow onion, peeled, halved, and thinly sliced

8 cloves garlic, peeled and crushed

3 tablespoons chili powder

1½ teaspoons kosher salt

1 teaspoon paprika

½ teaspoon ground black pepper

¼ cup tomato paste

4 cups low-sodium chicken broth

1 cup frozen sweet corn kernels

1 pound uncooked elbow macaroni pasta

1 (15-ounce) can kidney beans, drained and rinsed

12 ounces shredded mild Cheddar cheese

1 Place the insert in the 6-quart Instant Pot®. Press the Sauté button and select High/More. Once hot, add oil, ground beef, onion, garlic, and spices. Sauté 5 minutes, stirring occasionally, or until beef is mostly cooked through and onions begin to soften. Press Cancel to turn off Instant Pot®.

2 Add tomato paste, broth, corn, and pasta to pot. Stir to make sure that all the pasta is submerged under broth mixture.

3 Close lid, press the Manual or Pressure Cook button, and set time to 5 minutes at High Pressure. When the timer beeps, immediately quick-release the pressure until the float valve drops. Press the Cancel button and open lid.

4 Stir in beans and cheese. Serve.

PER SERVING
Calories: 903 | Fat: 39g | Protein: 48g | Sodium: 924mg | Fiber: 13g | Carbohydrates: 90g | Sugar: 5g

Hands-Off Homemade French Dip Sandwiches

SERVES
6

Homemade French dip sandwiches are usually an all-day affair. For this hands-off version, the Instant Pot® is used to quickly sear seasoned beef chuck roast, add select seasonings, and let the pressurized cooking environment create perfectly tender meat that is falling apart by the time the lid is opened.

> **PREP TIME: 3 MINUTES • ACTIVE COOK TIME: 10 MINUTES**
> **HANDS-OFF COOK TIME: 90 MINUTES (10 MINUTES TO PRESSURE +**
> **60 MINUTES COOKING TIME + 20 MINUTES NATURAL PRESSURE RELEASE)**

1 (3-pound) beef chuck roast, patted dry with paper towels

1 tablespoon kosher salt

1 teaspoon ground black pepper

2 tablespoons avocado oil

2 cups low-sodium beef broth

2 tablespoons low-sodium soy sauce

1/4 cup dried onion flakes

1 teaspoon onion powder

1/2 teaspoon dried parsley

1/2 teaspoon paprika

1/4 teaspoon celery seed

1 large yellow onion, peeled and cut into 8 wedges

1 dried bay leaf

12 (1-ounce) slices Swiss cheese

6 (6") pieces crusty baguette, sliced 3/4 way through

1 Place the insert in the 6-quart Instant Pot®. Press the Sauté button and select High/More. Place beef on a cutting board or dinner plate and rub with salt and pepper.

2 Once pot is heated up, add oil and seasoned beef. Sear 5 minutes per side (on the two largest sides). Press Cancel to turn off Instant Pot®.

3 Add broth, soy sauce, remaining spices, and onion wedges to pot, stir to combine, and add bay leaf. Close lid, press the Manual or Pressure Cook button, and set time to 60 minutes at High Pressure.

4 When the timer beeps, let pressure release naturally for 20 minutes, then quick-release remaining steam. Press the Cancel button and open lid.

Continued ▶

5 Remove bay leaf and discard. Remove beef to a cutting board and use two forks to shred beef and return to pot.

6 Layer 2 slices Swiss inside the top half of each baguette piece, leaving bottom to absorb some juices. Add shredded beef and serve sandwiches immediately with a small ramekin of cooking juice each for dipping.

PER SERVING
Calories: 756 | Fat: 41g | Protein: 64g | Sodium: 1,562mg | Fiber: 1g | Carbohydrates: 31g | Sugar: 1g

Tips, Substitutions, and More...

To save even more time, substitute a high-quality onion soup mix packet (like Simply Organic brand French onion dip mix) for all of the listed spices except for salt and pepper. Many people prefer provolone cheese in place of Swiss—both work great. If you have a few extra minutes, place cheese on the baguette and pop under the broiler for a few minutes before adding the beef.

Quick and Easy Pork Posole with Shredded Cabbage

SERVES 8

Pork posole is a traditional Mexican soup that features hominy (dried corn kernels treated with alkali), pork, chiles, and a collection of simple spices. The dish is most known for its rich and flavorful broth. Put the Instant Pot® to work to not only tenderize the meat but create a luscious broth in just over an hour—all hands-off cooking time. Garnish with shredded cabbage, sliced radishes, lime, cilantro, and avocado, then serve with corn tortillas for a satisfying bowl of goodness.

PREP TIME: 10 MINUTES ● ACTIVE COOK TIME: 5 MINUTES
HANDS-OFF COOK TIME: 70 MINUTES (20 MINUTES TO PRESSURE +
35 MINUTES COOKING TIME + 15 MINUTES NATURAL PRESSURE RELEASE)

2 tablespoons avocado oil

3 pounds pork stew meat (lean if possible), cut into 1" cubes

2 tablespoons chili powder

1 tablespoon ground cumin

1 tablespoon kosher salt

1 teaspoon ground black pepper

1 large yellow onion, peeled, halved, and thinly sliced

8 cloves garlic, peeled and smashed with back of a knife

1 medium poblano chile, seeded and chopped

4 cups low-sodium chicken broth

2 cups water

1 (27-ounce) can hominy, drained and rinsed

1 (15-ounce) can pinto beans, drained and rinsed

1 (12-ounce) jar salsa verde

Continued ▶

1   Place the insert in the 6-quart Instant Pot®. Press the Sauté button and select High/More. Once hot, add oil and a single layer of pork along with spices, onion, garlic, and poblano. Sauté 5 minutes, stirring occasionally.

2   Press Cancel to turn off Instant Pot®. Add remaining pork, broth, and water to pot. Close lid, press the Manual or Pressure Cook button, and set time to 35 minutes at High Pressure. When the timer beeps, let pressure release naturally for 15 minutes, then quick-release remaining steam.

Continued ▶

1 cup whole fresh cilantro leaves

1 (12-ounce) bag shredded green cabbage

4 medium radishes, thinly sliced

2 large avocados, peeled, pitted, and diced

2 medium limes, quartered

16 small (6") corn tortillas, warmed

3 Press the Cancel button, open lid, and stir in hominy, beans, and salsa verde. Serve in bowls topped with cilantro, cabbage, radish, avocado, and a squeeze of lime, with corn tortillas on the side.

PER SERVING
Calories: 552 | Fat: 20g | Protein: 42g | Sodium: 1,302mg | Fiber: 13g | Carbohydrates: 51g | Sugar: 7g

Tips, Substitutions, and More...

For a spicier version, swap two jalapeño peppers for the poblano.
In a pinch, omit corn tortillas and serve with tortilla chips.

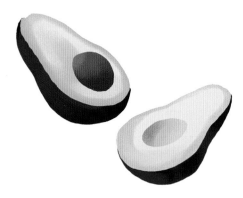

CHAPTER NINE

SOUP POT SUPPERS

While a large soup pot is an excellent vessel for soup, it can be used for so much more! The depth of a soup pot prevents liquid from cooking down too quickly, and the wide base allows for even sautéing and heat distribution.

In this chapter, you will find complete meals made in a soup pot that range from hearty soups like Creamy Tortellini Soup with Ground Beef, substantial stews like Portuguese Caldo Verde Stew, protein and vegetable curries like Spicy Thai Green Curry Shrimp with Vegetables, and even One Pot Angel Hair Pasta with Crabmeat and Chives. All of the following soup recipes are for thicker soups with lots of flavor and texture, so they will satisfy the family as a complete meal.

One Pot Angel Hair Pasta with Crabmeat and Chives

SERVES
6

This One Pot Angel Hair Pasta with Crabmeat and Chives looks and tastes super fancy but is actually one of the quickest recipes in this book from start to finish. The key is to buy a container of lump crabmeat or even jumbo lump crabmeat. Combine with quick-cooking angel hair pasta, a few spices, and thinly sliced fresh chives for an easy dinner that rivals any restaurant's.

PREP TIME: 5 MINUTES • ACTIVE COOK TIME: 10 MINUTES • HANDS-OFF COOK TIME: N/A

2 tablespoons plus $1/2$ teaspoon kosher salt, divided

1 pound uncooked angel hair pasta

1 cup reserved pasta cooking water

2 tablespoons extra-virgin olive oil

2 tablespoons salted butter

1 shallot, peeled, halved, and thinly sliced

$1/4$ teaspoon ground black pepper

$1/4$ teaspoon crushed red pepper flakes

1 (8-ounce) bottle clam juice

$1/2$ cup heavy cream

16 ounces lump crabmeat

$1/2$ cup thinly sliced chives

1 Fill a 6-quart or larger soup pot with 2" cold water and 2 tablespoons salt. Set over high heat and bring to a boil.

2 Once boiling, add pasta, cook for half of the recommended cooking time on the package (about 2–3 minutes), gently stirring until all pasta is submerged in water.

3 Use a glass measuring cup or mug to reserve 1 cup of pasta cooking water and set aside. Strain pasta in a colander and set aside to drain.

4 Return pot to stovetop over medium-high heat. Add oil and butter. Once hot, add shallot, remaining $1/2$ teaspoon salt, and spices, and cook 2 minutes, stirring continuously.

Continued ▶

5 Add clam juice and bring to a boil. Immediately add heavy cream and $1/2$ cup reserved pasta water. Stir to combine and add strained pasta to pot. Use tongs to gently toss pasta in sauce until most of it is absorbed into pasta, about 2 minutes. Add more reserved pasta water if needed.

6 Gently fold in crabmeat and chives and warm through, about 1 minute. Serve immediately.

PER SERVING
Calories: 505 | Fat: 19g | Protein: 28g | Sodium: 1,432mg | Fiber: 3g | Carbohydrates: 55g | Sugar: 3g

Tips, Substitutions, and More...

Seafood stock or dry white wine can be substituted for clam juice. Serve topped with freshly cracked black pepper. For a bit more heat, increase the crushed red pepper flakes to $1/2$ teaspoon.

Turmeric Chicken and Rice Soup

SERVES 6

This soul-soothing Turmeric Chicken and Rice Soup reduces prep work by combining already shredded rotisserie chicken and frozen crinkle cut carrot rounds with celery, onion, and the anti-inflammatory benefits of turmeric. The jasmine rice cooks directly in the broth, eliminating the need for a second pot and delivering a rich and thick soup that eats like a stew.

PREP TIME: 8 MINUTES • ACTIVE COOK TIME: 5 MINUTES • HANDS-OFF COOK TIME: 25 MINUTES

2 tablespoons extra-virgin olive oil

1 medium yellow onion, peeled, quartered, and thinly sliced

2 medium stalks celery, diced

2 cups frozen crinkle cut carrot rounds

2^1/2 teaspoons kosher salt

1 teaspoon dried thyme

^{1}/2 teaspoon ground black pepper

^{1}/2 teaspoon ground turmeric

^{1}/2 teaspoon dried sage

8 cups low-sodium chicken broth

1 pound shredded rotisserie chicken

^{1}/2 cup uncooked jasmine rice, rinsed

1 Place a 6-quart or larger soup pot over medium-high heat. Once hot, add oil, onion, celery, carrots, and spices. Sauté 5 minutes, stirring occasionally, or until onions begin to soften.

2 Add broth and bring to a boil. Once boiling, add chicken and rice. Cover, reduce heat to a strong simmer (medium-low), and cook undisturbed 25 minutes or until rice if fully cooked and soup has thickened. Serve.

PER SERVING
Calories: 330 | Fat: 17g | Protein: 20g | Sodium: 1,478mg | Fiber: 1g | Carbohydrates: 24g | Sugar: 1g

Tips, Substitutions, and More...

Increase rice to ^{3}/4 cup for a thicker version. If adding frozen shredded rotisserie chicken, add along with broth before it comes to a boil. No rotisserie chicken on hand? Add 1 pound uncooked boneless, skinless chicken breast along with broth before bringing to a boil. Remove cooked chicken when soup is done, then shred with two forks and return to soup pot before serving. Basmati rice can be substituted for the jasmine rice.

20-Minute Steamed Mussels with Buttered Peas

SERVES 4

Don't be intimidated by fresh mussels. Most commercially available fresh mussels are farm-raised, which means they are actually very clean in terms of sand and grit. Just spend a few minutes looking over them for broken mussels and pull off any long beards. Then combine with shallots, garlic, spices, white wine, and frozen peas. Just 10 minutes later, you have a seafood feast that is fantastic with crusty bread for dipping!

PREP TIME: 15 MINUTES • ACTIVE COOK TIME: 10 MINUTES • HANDS-OFF COOK TIME: N/A

5 pounds fresh mussels in shells, cleaned and debearded

2 tablespoons extra-virgin olive oil

4 tablespoons salted butter, divided

8 cloves garlic, peeled and crushed

2 shallots, peeled and thinly sliced

1/2 teaspoon crushed red pepper flakes

1/4 teaspoon freshly ground black pepper

1 cup dry white wine

1 (1-pound) bag frozen peas

1/4 cup finely chopped fresh flat-leaf parsley

1 (12-ounce) white baguette, sliced, toasted

1. Place mussels in a large mixing bowl and cover with 3–4 cups of ice while you prepare remaining ingredients.

2. Place a 6-quart or larger soup pot over medium-high heat. Once hot, add oil, 2 tablespoons butter, garlic, shallots, red pepper flakes, and black pepper. Sauté 1 minute, stirring constantly, or until garlic is fragrant.

3. Add wine to pot, bring to boil, and reduce by half, once boiling (about 3 minutes).

4. Add peas and drained mussels, cover, and cook 4–6 minutes until mussels have opened.

5. Turn off heat. Stir in parsley and remaining 2 tablespoons butter. Serve immediately with sliced baguette for dipping.

PER SERVING
Calories: 667 | Fat: 24g | Protein: 38g | Sodium: 911g | Fiber: 6g | Carbohydrates: 74g | Sugar: 6g

Tips, Substitutions, and More...

To clean mussels, place them in a large bowl and fill with very cold water. Swish around to remove dirt and sand. Give the mussels a once-over and pull off any "beards" (stringy pieces hanging off sides where the mussel closes) by pulling the beard downward and removing. Strain mussels from water.

Spicy Thai Green Curry Shrimp with Vegetables

SERVES 4

The secret to making a complex and delicious Thai Green Curry Shrimp with Vegetables in under 15 minutes is using a high-quality green curry paste, already peeled and deveined shrimp, and convenience vegetables. This recipe combines frozen mixed bell pepper strips and sliced fresh mushrooms with cleaned and trimmed green beans. The only prep work is halving the green beans, crushing garlic, and measuring ingredients.

PREP TIME: 5 MINUTES • ACTIVE COOK TIME: 8 MINUTES • HANDS-OFF COOK TIME: N/A

2 tablespoons avocado oil

1/4 cup green curry paste

4 cloves garlic, peeled and crushed

1 (13.5-ounce) can full-fat coconut milk

2 teaspoons granulated sugar

1 teaspoon fish sauce

1/4 teaspoon kosher salt

1 1/2 pounds uncooked, peeled, deveined large shrimp, fresh or defrosted and drained

8 ounces frozen mixed bell pepper strips

1 (10-ounce) package sliced white mushrooms

8 ounces cleaned and trimmed green beans, cut in half

10 fresh basil leaves

3 cups reheated precooked white rice

1 Place a 6-quart or larger soup pot over medium-high heat. Once hot, add oil, curry paste, and garlic. Stir continuously, until garlic becomes aromatic, 30 seconds.

2 Immediately add coconut milk, sugar, fish sauce, and salt. Stir until completely dissolved, approximately 2 minutes.

3 Add shrimp, bell peppers, mushrooms, and green beans. Cover and simmer 5 minutes or until shrimp are cooked through.

4 Remove from heat, stir in basil leaves, and serve immediately alongside rice.

PER SERVING
Calories: 878 | Fat: 35g | Protein: 43g | Sodium: 1,342mg | Fiber: 4g | Carbohydrates: 98g | Sugar: 18g

Tips, Substitutions, and More...

For an even hotter version, add a thinly sliced serrano pepper or Thai chile to the curry along with the shrimp. Not a fan of spice? Swap for yellow or massaman curry paste. If using frozen peeled and deveined shrimp, make sure that they are fully defrosted and drained of any excess liquid.

Split Pea Soup with Smoked Sausage

Many traditional split pea soup recipes are made with ham hocks or bacon. While both are very delicious, to save time and effort, this recipe utilizes crumbled smoked sausage for that smoky and rich flavor in every bite. Serve topped with your favorite crunchy croutons for texture.

PREP TIME: 15 MINUTES • ACTIVE COOK TIME: 7 MINUTES • HANDS-OFF COOK TIME: 105 MINUTES

2 tablespoons extra-virgin olive oil

1 pound uncooked smoked kielbasa, crumbled

1 large yellow onion, peeled and diced

4 cloves garlic, peeled and crushed

4 medium stalks celery, diced

1$\frac{1}{2}$ teaspoons kosher salt

1 teaspoon dried thyme

$\frac{1}{2}$ teaspoon ground black pepper

8 cups low-sodium chicken broth

1 pound dried green split peas

1 dried bay leaf

2 cups frozen crinkle cut carrot rounds

$\frac{3}{4}$ cup croutons

1 Place a 6-quart or larger soup pot over medium-high heat. Once hot, add oil, kielbasa, onion, garlic, celery, and spices. Sauté, stirring occasionally, 5 minutes or until vegetables begin to soften and kielbasa is mostly cooked through.

2 Keeping heat set to medium-high, add broth, split peas, and bay leaf, and bring to a boil. Once boiling, cover, reduce heat to a medium-low simmer, and cook 75 minutes, stirring occasionally.

3 Remove lid, add carrots, and simmer uncovered over medium heat 30 minutes or until carrots and peas are tender and soup has thickened up. Remove and discard bay leaf. Serve topped with croutons.

PER SERVING
Calories: 344 | Fat: 24g | Protein: 16g | Sodium: 1,028mg | Fiber: 2g | Carbohydrates: 16g | Sugar: 4g

Tips, Substitutions, and More...

Any type of uncooked smoked pork sausage can be substituted. This soup continues to thicken as it sits. To reheat leftover soup, you may need to add 1–2 tablespoons chicken broth to loosen it up. To save even more time, look for a container or bag of already diced onions at the grocery store.

Pearl Couscous with Sausage and Peppers

SERVES 6

Weeknight dinners have never been easier. Combine quick-cooking pearl couscous with Italian sausage, frozen mixed bell pepper slices, thick-cut yellow onion, and your favorite high-quality marinara sauce for a dinner that is loaded with flavor and texture!

PREP TIME: 5 MINUTES • ACTIVE COOK TIME: 22 MINUTES • HANDS-OFF COOK TIME: N/A

2 tablespoons extra-virgin olive oil

1$\frac{1}{2}$ pounds bulk uncooked mild Italian sausage

1 large yellow onion, peeled, halved, and cut into $\frac{1}{8}$" slices

3 cups low-sodium chicken broth

2 cups uncooked pearl couscous

1 (24-ounce) jar marinara sauce

1 (1-pound) bag frozen mixed bell pepper strips

1   Place a 6-quart or larger soup pot over medium-high heat. Once hot, add oil, sausage, and onion. Sauté 5 minutes, using a spatula to break sausage into pieces, or until sausage is mostly cooked through and onions begin to soften.

2   Add broth and bring to a boil. Once boiling, add couscous, cover, reduce heat to medium, and simmer 10 minutes, stirring occasionally to prevent sticking.

3   Remove lid and stir in marinara sauce and bell peppers. Continue cooking 5 minutes, stirring frequently, or until peppers are warmed through and couscous has finished cooking. Serve.

PER SERVING
Calories: 628 | Fat: 34g | Protein: 28g | Sodium: 1,301mg | Fiber: 3g | Carbohydrates: 52g | Sugar: 9g

Tips, Substitutions, and More...

To add some heat, substitute arrabbiata sauce for marinara, substitute hot Italian sausage for the mild, or add 1 teaspoon crushed red pepper flakes to marinara sauce. This dish is excellent served topped with grated Parmesan cheese.

Portuguese Caldo Verde Stew

The traditional version of caldo verde has a significant amount more prep work than this shortcut version. Here, you can skip chopping the onion and just halve and thinly slice it, which is a much quicker preparation. Additionally, butter potatoes are used in place of russet to avoid peeling. Lastly, look for a bag of already cleaned and chopped collard greens to make this a quick and easy one pot dinner that will warm your soul!

PREP TIME: 4 MINUTES • ACTIVE COOK TIME: 8 MINUTES • HANDS-OFF COOK TIME: 25 MINUTES

¼ cup extra-virgin olive oil

12 ounces bulk uncooked chorizo sausage, crumbled

1 large yellow onion, peeled, halved, and thinly sliced

2 teaspoons kosher salt

8 cups low-sodium chicken broth

2 pounds unpeeled Yukon Gold potatoes, cut into 1" chunks

1 (12-ounce) bag cleaned and chopped collard greens

Juice of ½ medium lemon

1. Place a 6-quart or larger soup pot over medium-high heat. Once hot, add oil and sausage. Cook, stirring occasionally and breaking up sausage with a wooden spoon or spatula, 3 minutes.

2. Add onion and salt. Continue sautéing 3 minutes, stirring occasionally. Add broth and potatoes, raise heat to high, and bring to a boil.

3. As soon as broth is boiling, immediately lower heat to medium and add collard greens. Continue cooking 25 minutes, stirring once or twice.

4. Remove about 10 chunks of potato to a soup bowl and use a fork to mash potato as fine as possible. Return mashed potato to soup, stir, and add lemon juice. Serve.

Tips, Substitutions, and More...

If you can't find bulk chorizo sausage or uncooked links to cut open and crumble, look for precooked links and cut them into chunks. Yukon Gold potatoes are often called "butter potatoes." If you can't find already cleaned and chopped collard greens, you can substitute cleaned and chopped kale.

PER SERVING

Calories: 555 | Fat: 33g | Protein: 25g | Sodium: 1,464mg | Fiber: 4g | Carbohydrates: 40g | Sugar: 4g

Old Bay Corn Chowder with Pancetta

This rich and comforting Old Bay Corn Chowder with Pancetta recipe saves you time and effort in the kitchen by relying on frozen sweet corn kernels, already diced pancetta, and cubed red potatoes that don't need to be peeled. Combine with the distinctive flavor of Old Bay seasoning, a few additional select spices, and the perfect amount of half-and-half for a velvety and rich broth that will make your family think this chowder took hours to make!

PREP TIME: 12 MINUTES • ACTIVE COOK TIME: 8 MINUTES • HANDS-OFF COOK TIME: 15 MINUTES

2 tablespoons salted butter

1 medium yellow onion, peeled and diced

2 cloves garlic, peeled and crushed

8 ounces diced pancetta

1 1/2 tablespoons Old Bay seasoning

1/2 teaspoon dried thyme

1/2 teaspoon kosher salt

1/4 teaspoon ground black pepper

1/4 cup all-purpose flour

4 cups low-sodium chicken broth

1 pound red potatoes, skin on, cut into 1/8s

1 1/2 cups frozen sweet corn kernels

1 dried bay leaf

1 cup half-and-half

3 medium scallions, thinly sliced

1 Place a 6-quart or larger soup pot over medium-high heat. Once hot, add butter, onion, garlic, pancetta, Old Bay seasoning, thyme, salt, and pepper. Sauté 5 minutes, stirring frequently, or until onions begin to soften. Add flour and sauté 1 minute, stirring constantly, or until flour begins to brown.

2 Add broth; use a spatula to scrape the bottom of the pot until smooth. Add potatoes, corn, and bay leaf; bring to a boil.

3 Once boiling, reduce heat to medium and simmer uncovered, stirring occasionally, 15 minutes or until potatoes are tender.

4 Turn off heat and remove bay leaf. Slowly stir in half-and-half (so it doesn't curdle). Serve in bowls topped with scallions.

PER SERVING
Calories: 376 | Fat: 24g | Protein: 14g | Sodium: 423mg | Fiber: 3g | Carbohydrates: 29g | Sugar: 6g

Brown Lentil and Sausage Stew with Kale

This Brown Lentil and Sausage Stew with Kale is a hearty dish that marries the earthy flavors of brown lentils, savory sausage, and kale. The stew is made with several time-saving ingredients, including quick-cooking sausage that doesn't need any cutting or chopping, canned tomatoes, and, of course, a bag of cleaned and chopped kale leaves.

PREP TIME: 10 MINUTES • ACTIVE COOK TIME: 7 MINUTES • HANDS-OFF COOK TIME: 25 MINUTES

1/4 cup extra-virgin olive oil

1 pound bulk uncooked mild Italian sausage

1 medium yellow onion, peeled, quartered, and thinly sliced

4 medium stalks celery, cut into 1/8" half-moons

4 cloves garlic, peeled and crushed

1 teaspoon smoked paprika

1 teaspoon ground oregano

1/2 teaspoon ground cumin

2 1/4 teaspoons kosher salt

6 cups low-sodium chicken broth

1 (15-ounce) can diced no-salt tomatoes

2 cups uncooked brown lentils, rinsed

6 ounces cleaned and chopped fresh kale

1 Place a 6-quart or larger soup pot over medium-high heat. Once hot, add oil, sausage, onion, celery, garlic, and spices. Sauté 5 minutes, stirring occasionally and breaking up sausage with a wooden spoon or spatula, or until onions begin to soften and most sausage is browned.

2 Keeping the heat set to medium-high, add broth, tomatoes, lentils, and kale, and bring to a boil. Once boiling, immediately reduce heat to medium and simmer uncovered 25 minutes or until lentils are tender, stirring occasionally. Serve.

PER SERVING
Calories: 506 | Fat: 22g | Protein: 31g | Sodium: 842mg | Fiber: 16g | Carbohydrates: 469g | Sugar: 11g

Tips, Substitutions, and More...

Baby spinach can be swapped for kale if preferred. If you can't find brown lentils, substitute French lentils. Do not use green lentils as they have a much firmer texture when cooked and won't work for this stew. This recipe is excellent topped with finely chopped fresh parsley and with crusty bread and butter on the side.

Creamy Tortellini Soup with Ground Beef

SERVES 4

Creamy Tortellini Soup with Ground Beef is a rich and flavorful dish loaded with protein, vegetables, quick-cooking cheese tortellini, and the perfect mix of spices. Ready from start to finish in just 20 minutes, this one pot dinner is excellent served with a bit of grated Parmesan cheese sprinkled on top.

PREP TIME: 10 MINUTES • ACTIVE COOK TIME: 10 MINUTES • HANDS-OFF COOK TIME: N/A

2 tablespoons extra-virgin olive oil

1 pound 80% lean ground beef

1 medium yellow onion, peeled, halved, and thinly sliced

1/2 cup shredded carrots

2 teaspoons Italian seasoning

2 teaspoons kosher salt

1/2 teaspoon ground black pepper

1/4 teaspoon crushed red pepper flakes

1/4 cup all-purpose flour

8 cups low-sodium chicken broth

1 (14-ounce) can diced no-salt tomatoes

1 1/2 pounds uncooked refrigerated cheese tortellini

1 (5-ounce) bag fresh baby spinach

1 (15-ounce) can white beans, drained and rinsed

1 1/2 cups half-and-half

1/2 cup plus 4 teaspoons grated Parmesan cheese, divided

1 Place a 6-quart or larger soup pot over medium-high heat. Once hot, add oil, ground beef, onion, carrots, and spices. Cook, stirring occasionally and breaking up beef with a wooden spoon or spatula, 4 minutes or until most of the pink is gone.

2 Add flour and cook 2 minutes, stirring constantly, or until beginning to brown.

3 Add broth and tomatoes. Use a spatula to scrape the bottom of the pot. Raise heat to high and bring to a boil. Once boiling, add tortellini, spinach, and beans; bring back to a boil and cook 3 minutes.

4 Remove pot from heat and stir in half-and-half and 1/2 cup Parmesan. Serve topped with remaining Parmesan.

PER SERVING
Calories: 1,235 | Fat: 52g | Protein: 63g | Sodium: 1,325mg | Fiber: 15g | Carbohydrates: 129g | Sugar: 19g

Tips, Substitutions, and More…

Swap crumbled mild or hot Italian sausage for ground beef if preferred. Additionally, a frozen carrot and pea mixture is a great substitute for the shredded carrots. Add 3 minutes of cook time if using frozen tortellini.

CHAPTER TEN

WEEKNIGHT WOK WINS

The wok's origins can be traced back to ancient China, where it has been used for over 2,000 years. While woks are known for their versatility and can be used for a wide range of cooking techniques, including stir-frying, steaming, boiling, deep-frying, and more, this chapter focuses on stir-frying, as it is one of the quickest cooking methods.

In this chapter, you will find familiar recipes like Super Quick Beef and Broccoli, made with a time-saving shortcut of using ground beef instead of sliced and marinated steak. You will also learn how to make Shortcut Vegetable Lo Mein in just 15 minutes from start to finish and how to use your wok to create a Coconut Curry Noodle Soup with Shrimp in under 20 minutes that rivals takeout!

15-Minute Coconut Curry Noodle Soup with Shrimp

SERVES 6

In only 15 minutes, you can have a rich Coconut Curry Noodle Soup with Shrimp. Skip most of the prep work by using crushed garlic and snipping the scallions with kitchen scissors instead of chopping. Look for already peeled and deveined shrimp.

PREP TIME: 5 MINUTES ● ACTIVE COOK TIME: 10 MINUTES ● HANDS-OFF COOK TIME: N/A

2 tablespoons avocado oil

1/4 cup Thai red curry paste

4 cloves garlic, peeled and crushed

1/2 teaspoon ginger powder

8 cups low-sodium chicken broth

1 1/2 pounds frozen, uncooked, peeled, deveined large shrimp

1 (5-ounce) bag fresh baby spinach

1/4 cup coconut sugar

1 (13.5-ounce) can full-fat coconut milk

8 ounces uncooked vermicelli rice noodles

2 teaspoons fish sauce

Juice from 1 medium lime

4 medium scallions, thinly cut

1 cup fresh cilantro leaves, ripped apart

1. Heat a 14" or larger carbon steel wok over medium-high heat 2–3 minutes until hot. Once hot, add avocado oil and then curry paste, garlic, and ginger. Sauté 1 minute, whisking constantly to break up curry paste.

2. Add broth, raise heat to high, and bring to a boil, whisking until curry mixture is incorporated into broth. Once boiling, add shrimp, spinach, and sugar. Cook 2 minutes.

3. Whisk in coconut milk and add noodles. Cook 3 minutes.

4. Remove from heat; stir in fish sauce and lime juice. Serve topped with scallions and cilantro.

PER SERVING
Calories: 507 | Fat: 27g | Protein: 21g | Sodium: 130mg | Fiber: 1g | Carbohydrates: 45g | Sugar: 13g

Tips, Substitutions, and More...

Note that the noodles will swell as the soup sits. If you have some extra time, swap 1 tablespoon of fresh ginger for the ginger powder for a more pungent ginger flavor. Make sure to get uncooked, dried vermicelli rice noodles (very thin) for the best result.

Shortcut Vegetable Lo Mein

SERVES 4

Traditional lo mein noodles cook in less than 5 minutes, so instead of making a second pot dirty, you can cook them right in the wok and then turn around and start the sauce as the noodles drain. Combine quick-cooked noodles with a variety of prepared convenience vegetables and a 1-minute sauce, and you have "better than takeout" Shortcut Vegetable Lo Mein in a mere 15 minutes!

PREP TIME: 5 MINUTES • ACTIVE COOK TIME: 10 MINUTES • HANDS-OFF COOK TIME: N/A

1 pound uncooked lo mein noodles

1/4 cup low-sodium soy sauce

3 tablespoons hoisin sauce

2 tablespoons toasted sesame oil

4 teaspoons granulated sugar

1 teaspoon sriracha

1 teaspoon ground ginger

1/3 cup avocado oil

4 ounces snow peas

1 cup shredded carrots

1 cup shredded cabbage

1 (5-ounce) bag fresh baby spinach

Tips, Substitutions, and More…

If you can't find dry lo mein noodles, look for refrigerated already cooked lo mein or ramen noodles. Eliminate the boiling time and add already cooked noodles to wok in Step 6. Swap a slaw mix for the shredded cabbage and carrots to save even more time. And for additional protein, toss in shredded rotisserie chicken in Step 5.

1 Fill a 14" or larger carbon steel wok halfway with cold water. Set over high heat and bring water to a boil.

2 Add lo mein noodles to boiling water. Cook 5 minutes (or according to package directions).

3 While noodles are cooking, combine soy sauce, hoisin sauce, sesame oil, sugar, sriracha, and ginger in a glass measuring cup or small bowl. Set aside.

4 Carefully drain noodles and set aside in a colander.

5 Return wok to high heat and allow to heat 30 seconds to cook off any excess water. Once dry, add avocado oil and gently swirl to coat. Add snow peas, carrots, cabbage, and spinach. Stir-fry 1 minute.

6 Add strained noodles and sauce. Continuously toss with tongs 1 minute or until sauce is evenly distributed over noodles and vegetables. Serve immediately.

PER SERVING
Calories: 711 | Fat: 27g | Protein: 16g | Sodium: 1,413mg | Fiber: 7g | Carbohydrates: 101g | Sugar: 23g

Honey Soy Chicken Thighs with Snow Peas

SERVES 4

Start by making a simple sauce, preparing your chicken, and gathering snow peas. Then, just stir-fry everything together and serve with some warmed precooked rice. To save even more time, look in the grocery store for already sliced chicken breast or thighs. Or, you could even swap ground chicken or pork for the sliced chicken thighs.

PREP TIME: 10 MINUTES • ACTIVE COOK TIME: 12 MINUTES • HANDS-OFF COOK TIME: N/A

½ cup low-sodium soy sauce

¼ cup honey

2 tablespoons cornstarch

¾ teaspoon ginger powder

¼ teaspoon crushed red pepper flakes

4 cloves garlic, peeled and crushed

¼ cup avocado oil

1½ pounds boneless, skinless chicken thighs, cut into ½" strips

12 ounces snow peas

3 cups reheated precooked white rice

1 In a glass measuring cup or small bowl, combine soy sauce, honey, cornstarch, ginger, red pepper flakes, and garlic until well mixed; set aside.

2 Heat a 14" or larger carbon steel wok over high heat 1–2 minutes until hot. Once hot, add oil and chicken. Cook undisturbed 3 minutes, then toss chicken to turn and continue cooking another 3 minutes, stirring occasionally.

3 Add sauce to wok and bring to a boil, about 1 minute. Immediately add snow peas and toss until chicken and snow peas are well coated with sauce, about 45 seconds.

4 Remove from heat and serve immediately alongside rice.

PER SERVING
Calories: 828 | Fat: 31g | Protein: 42g | Sodium: 1,430mg | Fiber: 3g | Carbohydrates: 95g | Sugar: 22g

Tips, Substitutions, and More…

If you substitute broccoli florets, trimmed green beans, or sugar snap peas for the snow peas, you need to adjust the cook time and add them before adding the sauce so that they don't break from cooking too long. For a spicy version, double the crushed garlic and increase crushed red pepper flakes to 1 teaspoon.

Ground Beef Stir-Fry with Bean Sprouts and Scallions

SERVES 4

Ground Beef Stir-Fry is the perfect answer for busy nights. There is no chopping required: Just mix some sauce ingredients together in a small bowl, and gather ground beef, frozen stir-fry vegetable mix, a bag of bean sprouts, and some scallions. Use kitchen scissors to cut the scallions without dirtying a cutting board and knife.

PREP TIME: 5 MINUTES • ACTIVE COOK TIME: 10 MINUTES • HANDS-OFF COOK TIME: N/A

1/4 cup water

1/4 cup low-sodium soy sauce

1/4 cup packed light brown sugar

1 tablespoon sriracha

1 1/2 teaspoons ground ginger

1/4 teaspoon ground black pepper

1 tablespoon cornstarch

6 cloves garlic, peeled and crushed

1 (1-pound) bag frozen stir-fry vegetable blend

2 tablespoons avocado oil

1 1/2 pounds 80% lean ground beef

1 (8-ounce) package bean sprouts

6 medium scallions, cut into 1" pieces

3 cups reheated precooked white rice

1 In a glass measuring cup or small bowl, combine water, soy sauce, sugar, sriracha, ginger, pepper, cornstarch, and garlic. Set aside.

2 Set a 14" or larger carbon steel wok over high heat until just beginning to smoke, about 2 minutes. Once hot, add stir-fry vegetable blend, cover, and cook undisturbed 2 minutes.

3 Remove cover, stir, and cook an additional 1 minute or until warmed through and liquid has begun pooling. Transfer vegetable mix to a strainer and return wok to high heat. Allow wok to heat 30 seconds to cook off any excess water.

4 Add oil and ground beef to wok. Cook 4 minutes, using a spatula to break up beef into large chunks, or until most of the pink is gone.

Tips, Substitutions, and More...

Not a fan of beef? You can use ground pork or chicken instead. For a spicy version, increase the sriracha to 2 tablespoons. Don't feel like rice or want a lower-carb version? Spoon the stir-fry into iceberg lettuce leaves to make wraps.

5 Add vegetable mix to the beef mixture, stir to combine, and add sauce. Bring to a boil, tossing ingredients and stirring constantly, about 90 seconds.

6 As soon as sauce is bubbling, add bean sprouts and scallions. Toss 1 minute. Turn off heat and serve immediately over rice.

PER SERVING
Calories: 927 | Fat: 41g | Protein: 39g | Sodium: 830mg | Fiber: 2g | Carbohydrates: 101g | Sugar: 3g

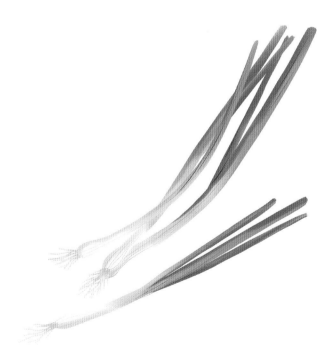

Thai Red Curry Pork Stir-Fry with Green Beans

SERVES 4

A simple, flavor-packed weeknight stir-fry capitalizing on the ease of ground pork, jarred curry paste, and already cleaned and trimmed green beans!

PREP TIME: 5 MINUTES ● ACTIVE COOK TIME: 8 MINUTES ● HANDS-OFF COOK TIME: N/A

1/2 cup low-sodium chicken broth

2 1/2 tablespoons granulated sugar

1 teaspoon fish sauce

1 tablespoon cornstarch

2 tablespoons avocado oil

1 1/2 pounds 85% lean ground pork

1/4 cup Thai red curry paste

1 (1-pound) package cleaned and trimmed green beans, cut in half

3 cups reheated precooked white rice

4 medium scallions, sliced

1 medium lime, cut into quarters

1. In a glass measuring cup or small bowl, combine broth, sugar, fish sauce, and cornstarch. Set aside.

2. Heat a 14" or larger carbon steel wok over high heat 1–2 minutes until hot. Once hot, add oil, ground pork, and curry paste. Use a spatula to mix until pork is coated with curry paste. Continue stir-frying 3 minutes, stirring occasionally.

3. Add green beans, cover, and cook 2 minutes undisturbed.

4. Remove cover, add sauce, toss until pork and green beans are well coated and sauce begins to thicken, about 90 seconds to 2 minutes.

5. Remove and serve alongside rice, topped with scallions and a squeeze of lime juice.

PER SERVING
Calories: 807 | Fat: 33g | Protein: 40g | Sodium: 98mg | Fiber: 5g | Carbohydrates: 88g | Sugar: 12g

Tips, Substitutions, and More...
All curry paste brands vary in terms of saltiness and spiciness. Try a commonly found brand like Thai Kitchen.

Kimchi Beef Stir-Fry with Water Chestnuts

SERVES
4

A little-known secret is that most grocery store butcher departments will slice your meat for you if you ask them nicely or, even better, call in the morning and give them ample time to fulfill the request. Either way, this stir-fry is worth the extra few minutes if you wind up slicing it yourself. The combination of sliced beef, crunchy water chestnuts, tangy kimchi, and scallions is really, really tasty!

PREP TIME: 14 MINUTES • ACTIVE COOK TIME: 6 MINUTES • HANDS-OFF COOK TIME: N/A

2 tablespoons cornstarch

1 1/2 teaspoons kosher salt

1 teaspoon ground ginger

1/2 teaspoon ground black pepper

1 1/2 pounds beef sirloin steak, fat trimmed, thinly sliced against the grain

1/2 cup kimchi (with juice), packed

2 tablespoons low-sodium soy sauce

1 teaspoon apple cider vinegar

1 (8-ounce) can sliced water chestnuts, drained

2 tablespoons avocado oil

1 (8-ounce) bag shredded cabbage

4 medium scallions, sliced into 1/2" pieces on the diagonal

3 cups reheated precooked white rice

1 On a cutting board, sprinkle cornstarch, salt, ginger, and pepper on beef and toss until cornstarch and spices are incorporated into beef. Set cutting board aside.

2 In a glass measuring cup, combine kimchi, soy sauce, apple cider vinegar, and water chestnuts. Set aside.

3 Heat a 14" or larger carbon steel wok over high heat until just beginning to smoke, about 2 minutes. Once hot, add oil and beef. Use a spatula to separate the beef and cook undisturbed 2 minutes.

4 Toss beef and cook an additional 2 minutes. Add cabbage, toss, and cook 1 minute. Add kimchi mixture, toss, and cook 1 more minute.

5 Remove from heat, add scallions, and serve immediately over rice.

PER SERVING
Calories: 564 | Fat: 12g | Protein: 33g | Sodium: 1,210mg | Fiber: 3g | Carbohydrates: 80g | Sugar: 3g

Copycat Chicken Lettuce Wraps

While there are many versions of Asian-style chicken and vegetable lettuce wraps out there, this copycat recipe swaps ground chicken for diced chicken to save significant prep time. Besides crushing a few cloves of garlic, the remaining prep is gathering and measuring ingredients to deliver an unbelievably tasty restaurant-style dinner in just over 12 minutes start to finish!

PREP TIME: 5 MINUTES • ACTIVE COOK TIME: 8 MINUTES • HANDS-OFF COOK TIME: N/A

1/4 cup hoisin sauce

1 tablespoon toasted sesame oil

2 teaspoons sriracha

2 tablespoons avocado oil

1 pound ground chicken breast

4 cloves garlic, peeled and crushed

1/2 teaspoon ginger powder

1 teaspoon kosher salt

2/3 cup frozen peas

1/2 cup shredded carrots

1 (8-ounce) can diced water chestnuts, drained

1 large head iceberg lettuce, leaves separated

1. In a glass measuring cup or small bowl, mix hoisin sauce, sesame oil, and sriracha. Set aside.

2. Heat a 14" or larger carbon steel wok over high heat 1–2 minutes until hot. Once hot, add avocado oil and ground chicken. Cook undisturbed 3 minutes.

3. Add garlic, ginger, and salt and toss chicken; cook 1 more minute. Add peas, carrots, and water chestnuts. Toss and cook 2 minutes.

4. Add sauce and cook 1 minute to heat through and thicken. Turn off heat and toss until sauce is completely incorporated, about 30 seconds. Serve with lettuce leaves for wrapping.

PER SERVING
Calories: 156 | Fat: 7g | Protein: 14g | Sodium: 461mg | Fiber: 2g | Carbohydrates: 9g | Sugar: 5g

Tips, Substitutions, and More…

Swap a mix of frozen peas and carrots for the frozen peas and refrigerated shredded carrots. If you can't find canned diced water chestnuts, look for sliced water chestnuts and roughly chop them after draining. For a spicy version, serve with hot chili oil or double the sriracha in the sauce. Ground pork or dark meat ground chicken can be swapped for the ground chicken breast.

Super Quick Beef and Broccoli

SERVES 4

When it comes to classic Beef and Broccoli, the things that take the most time are correctly slicing the sirloin or steak, creating the marinade, and resting the beef before cooking. This super quick version eliminates all of those steps by swapping in ground beef! This dinner is on the table in just 15 minutes.

PREP TIME: 5 MINUTES • ACTIVE COOK TIME: 10 MINUTES • HANDS-OFF COOK TIME: N/A

For Sauce

1/2 cup low-sodium soy sauce

2 tablespoons granulated sugar

1 tablespoon cornstarch

1 tablespoon toasted sesame oil

3 cloves garlic, peeled and crushed

1/4 teaspoon ginger powder

1/4 teaspoon crushed red pepper flakes

1 To make Sauce: In a glass measuring cup or small bowl, combine all ingredients. Set aside.

For Beef and Broccoli

1 1/2 pounds 80% lean ground beef

1/2 teaspoon baking soda

2 tablespoons avocado oil

1 (1-pound) bag fresh broccoli florets

3 cups reheated precooked white rice

2 To make Beef and Broccoli: Place ground beef onto a dinner plate. Sprinkle baking soda over meat and use your hands to fold it in. Set aside.

3 Preheat a 14" or larger carbon steel wok over high heat 1–2 minutes until hot. Once hot, add avocado oil and ground beef. Cook undisturbed 2 minutes. Toss beef and continue cooking 2 more minutes, or until most of the pink is gone.

Continued ▶

4 Add broccoli, stir to combine, cover, and cook 4 minutes.

5 Remove the lid, add sauce, and cook undisturbed 1 minute. Toss until beef and broccoli are well coated with sauce and serve immediately over rice.

PER SERVING
Calories: 904 | Fat: 44g | Protein: 39g | Sodium: 1,453mg | Fiber: 6g | Carbohydrates: 88g | Sugar: 10g

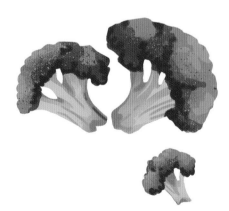

CHAPTER ELEVEN

DUMP AND GO SLOW COOKER MEALS

When it comes to slow cooker recipes, it's important to acknowledge that while the cook time is long, the prep time is minimal. The beautiful part about the slow cooker is that you can set it and forget it. Pop it on early in the morning and ignore it, then come back around dinnertime to a wonderful and complex meal that is ready to eat!

In this chapter, you'll find delicious meals like Red Beans and Rice with Smoked Sausage, Creamy Buffalo Blue Cheese Chicken Sandwiches, and Hoisin Pulled Pork Rice Bowls with Cucumbers. Most the recipes that follow have just 10 minutes or less of active prep time, so you can spend less time in the kitchen and more time on the important things.

Mixed Bean and Corn Chili with Butternut Squash

SERVES
6

This vegetarian Mixed Bean and Corn Chili with Butternut Squash is a comforting and hearty meal made 100% in the slow cooker without any active cooking time. Just layer the ingredients in the order listed, set it (the slow cooker), and forget it. The end result is a wholesome chili filled with a medley of beans, sweet corn, and cubed butternut squash. Perfect with your favorite chili toppings and a side of tortilla chips!

PREP TIME: 15 MINUTES • ACTIVE COOK TIME: N/A • HANDS-OFF COOK TIME: 7 HOURS ON LOW

2 tablespoons avocado oil

1 cup low-sodium vegetable broth

1 (28-ounce) can crushed tomatoes

1 (4-ounce) can diced green chiles

1 medium yellow onion, peeled and diced

2 medium stalks celery, diced

4 cloves garlic, peeled and crushed

1 tablespoon kosher salt

1 tablespoon plus 1 teaspoon chili powder

2 teaspoons ground cumin

1 teaspoon smoked paprika

1 teaspoon dried oregano

1/4 teaspoon cayenne pepper

1 (15-ounce) can black beans, drained and rinsed

1 (15-ounce) can kidney beans, drained and rinsed

1 (15-ounce) can pinto beans, drained and rinsed

1 (1-pound) bag frozen cubed butternut squash

1 1/2 cups frozen sweet corn kernels

1 Add all ingredients to the insert of a 6-quart or larger slow cooker in order listed and stir to combine.

2 Cover with lid and set to low for 7 hours. Serve.

PER SERVING
Calories: 426 | Fat: 7g | Protein: 23g | Sodium: 1,245mg | Fiber: 23g | Carbohydrates: 68g | Sugar: 10g

Tips, Substitutions, and More...

To cook faster, set the slow cooker to high for 4 1/2 hours. Swap fresh cubed squash for frozen if it is in season. Some topping ideas include shredded cheese, sour cream, cilantro, scallions, tortilla chips, hot sauce, and pickled jalapeños.

Chicken Adobo Bowls with Snow Peas

SERVES
6

This completely hands-off take on chicken adobo tastes amazing and is ridiculously easy to make. The chicken is slow cooked all day in a savory sauce inspired by the bold flavors of Filipino adobo. Pair with crunchy steamed snow peas over a bed of rice.

PREP TIME: 5 MINUTES • ACTIVE COOK TIME: N/A • HANDS-OFF COOK TIME: 7½ HOURS ON LOW

½ cup white vinegar

½ cup low-sodium soy sauce

1 cup low-sodium chicken broth

1 (3") piece fresh ginger, cut in half through the middle

8 cloves garlic, peeled and smashed with back of a knife

4 dried bay leaves

20 whole black peppercorns

2½ pounds boneless, skinless chicken thighs

1 pound snow peas

4½ cups reheated precooked white rice

3 medium scallions, sliced

Tips, Substitutions, and More...

Take care to scoop out and discard the ginger, peppercorns, and bay leaves. Trimmed green beans or snap peas can be substituted for snow peas, but cooking time will increase by a few minutes. To cook faster, set slow cooker to high for 4 hours and decrease cooking time for snow peas to 3–4 minutes.

1 Add vinegar, soy sauce, broth, ginger, garlic, bay leaves, and peppercorns to the insert of a 6-quart or larger slow cooker. Stir to combine.

2 Nestle chicken thighs in sauce and use a spoon to spoon some sauce over the top of any chicken not submerged. Cover with lid and set to low for 7½ hours.

3 After 7 hours and 15 minutes, transfer chicken thighs to a cutting board. Use a slotted spoon to scoop ginger pieces, bay leaves, and peppercorns from sauce and discard.

4 Use a fork to shred chicken and return to sauce. Place snow peas on top of chicken mixture, trying to keep them above sauce. Place lid back on and continue with remaining 8 minutes of cooking time to soften and steam snow peas.

5 Immediately remove snow peas after 8 minutes so that they don't overcook. Serve shredded chicken and snow peas over rice, topped with sauce and scallions.

PER SERVING
Calories: 684 | Fat: 19g | Protein: 48g | Sodium: 1,011mg | Fiber: 3g | Carbohydrates: 80g | Sugar: 4g

Creamy Chicken Enchilada Soup

SERVES 6

Make this Creamy Chicken Enchilada Soup in minutes by layering all of the ingredients in the slow cooker. The only prep work is crushing garlic, dicing an onion (save even more time by buying already diced onion at the grocery store), rinsing beans, and measuring some spices. Place the whole uncooked chicken breasts right into the broth and let the slow cooker do the work.

PREP TIME: 10 MINUTES • ACTIVE COOK TIME: N/A • HANDS-OFF COOK TIME: 7 HOURS ON LOW

2 tablespoons avocado oil

1 tablespoon ground cumin

2 teaspoons kosher salt

1 medium yellow onion, peeled and diced

6 cloves garlic, peeled and crushed

1 (16-ounce) jar red enchilada sauce

4 cups low-sodium chicken broth

2 (15-ounce) cans pinto beans, drained and rinsed

1 1/2 cups frozen sweet corn kernels

1 pound boneless, skinless chicken breasts

1 (8-ounce) package full-fat cream cheese

1. In the insert of a 6-quart or larger slow cooker, combine oil, cumin, salt, onion, garlic, enchilada sauce, and broth.

2. Add beans and corn. Place chicken in broth mixture, submerging as much as possible. Finally, add cream cheese without stirring.

3. Cover with lid and set to low for 7 hours. When cooking time is up, transfer chicken to a cutting board and use two forks to shred.

4. Whisk cream cheese into soup broth until well mixed and return shredded chicken to soup. Serve.

PER SERVING
Calories: 607 | Fat: 32g | Protein: 40g | Sodium: 1,472mg | Fiber: 11g | Carbohydrates: 42g | Sugar: 7g

Tips, Substitutions, and More...

Some good toppings include shredded cheese, cilantro leaves, diced avocado, sliced scallions, thinly sliced jalapeños for heat, shredded green cabbage, and your favorite tortilla chips. To cook faster, set slow cooker to high for 3 1/2 hours.

Winner Winner Chicken Dinner

SERVES 4

Use your slow cooker to create a hassle-free chicken dinner with just 10 minutes of work. Throw in seasoned boneless, skinless chicken breasts; quartered red potatoes; and cleaned and trimmed green beans over a bed of shredded cabbage. Top with a jar of marinated artichokes, set it, and forget it. Come home to a satisfying and flavorful chicken dinner that practically made itself.

PREP TIME: 10 MINUTES • ACTIVE COOK TIME: N/A • HANDS-OFF COOK TIME: 7 HOURS

12 ounces shredded green cabbage

4 (8-ounce) boneless, skinless chicken breasts

3 tablespoons extra-virgin olive oil, divided

$1\frac{1}{2}$ teaspoons kosher salt, divided

$1\frac{1}{4}$ teaspoons dried oregano, divided

$\frac{3}{4}$ teaspoon ground black pepper, divided

$1\frac{1}{2}$ pounds red potatoes, quartered

1 (12-ounce) package cleaned and trimmed green beans

1 (12-ounce) jar marinated and quartered artichokes with juice

Tips, Substitutions, and More...

If the cabbage is cut very thin, it will almost disappear but still taste amazing. You can substitute boneless, skinless chicken thighs, trimmed of visible fat, for the chicken breasts if preferred.

1. Layer cabbage evenly on bottom of 6-quart or larger slow cooker insert.

2. Place chicken on a dinner plate or cutting board. Combine 1 tablespoon oil, $\frac{1}{2}$ teaspoon salt, $\frac{1}{2}$ teaspoon oregano, and $\frac{1}{4}$ teaspoon black pepper in a small bowl and rub evenly over all sides of chicken. Transfer chicken to middle section of slow cooker on top of cabbage.

3. In a large bowl, toss quartered potatoes with 1 tablespoon oil, $\frac{1}{2}$ teaspoon salt, $\frac{1}{2}$ teaspoon oregano, and $\frac{1}{4}$ teaspoon pepper. Transfer potatoes to slow cooker and stack to one side of the chicken.

4. In the same bowl, toss green beans with remaining 1 tablespoon oil, $\frac{1}{2}$ teaspoon salt, $\frac{1}{4}$ teaspoon oregano, and $\frac{1}{4}$ teaspoon pepper. Transfer to slow cooker and stack on opposite side of chicken. Pour artichokes and juice over chicken, green beans, and potatoes.

5. Cover with lid and set to low for 7 hours. Serve.

PER SERVING
Calories: 822 | Fat: 26g | Protein: 82g | Sodium: 1,254mg | Fiber: 16g | Carbohydrates: 65g | Sugar: 21g

Creamy Buffalo Blue Cheese Chicken Sandwiches

SERVES
8

Make life easy with these Creamy Buffalo Blue Cheese Chicken Sandwiches. Toss boneless, skinless chicken breasts into the slow cooker with Frank's RedHot and a brick of full-fat cream cheese. When the cooking time is up, quickly shred the chicken with two forks and serve on toasted sandwich rolls topped with crumbled blue cheese.

PREP TIME: 5 MINUTES • ACTIVE COOK TIME: N/A
HANDS-OFF COOK TIME: 7 HOURS 10 MINUTES, ON LOW

2 pounds boneless, skinless chicken breast

1 cup Frank's RedHot Original Cayenne Pepper Sauce

1 (8-ounce) package full-fat cream cheese

4 medium scallions, thinly sliced

8 (6") white sandwich rolls, toasted

4 ounces crumbled blue cheese

1 Combine chicken, hot sauce, and cream cheese in the insert of a 6-quart or larger slow cooker. Cover with lid and set to low for 7 hours.

2 Remove chicken to a cutting board and use two forks to shred.

3 Leaving hot sauce mixture in slow cooker, whisk hot sauce and cream cheese until well mixed. Add shredded chicken back to sauce. Allow to sit uncovered 10 minutes to naturally thicken, then stir in scallions.

4 Serve on sandwich rolls with blue cheese on top.

PER SERVING
Calories: 530 | Fat: 14g | Protein: 41g | Sodium: 1,902mg | Fiber: 1g | Carbohydrates: 60g | Sugar: 8g

Tips, Substitutions, and More...

To cook faster, set the slow cooker to high for 3⅓ hours. Swap boneless, skinless chicken thighs for chicken breasts if preferred. Not in the mood for sandwiches? Serve as lettuce wraps, over a baked potato, with warmed rice, or even as a dip with buttery crackers!

Red Beans and Rice with Smoked Sausage

SERVES
8

Create a delicious and satisfying dinner the whole family will love by combining dry red beans (no presoaking needed!), smoked sausage, broth, creole seasoning, onion, bell pepper, and garlic in the slow cooker. Hours later, a creamy and complex sauce laced with the smoky notes from the sausage will be the base for a no-fuss meal served over rice.

PREP TIME: 15 MINUTES • ACTIVE COOK TIME: N/A • HANDS-OFF COOK TIME: 8 HOURS

1 pound unsoaked dried small red beans, rinsed

2 tablespoons creole seasoning

1 dried bay leaf

1 medium yellow onion, peeled, halved, and thinly sliced

1 medium green bell pepper, seeds and ribs removed, diced

4 cloves garlic, peeled and smashed with back of knife

24 ounces smoked pork sausage (such as andouille, kielbasa, chorizo), cut into 1/2"-thick rounds

6 cups low-sodium chicken broth

6 cups reheated precooked white rice

1 Add all ingredients except rice to the insert of a 6-quart or larger slow cooker. Stir to mix well.

2 Cover with lid and set to high for 8 hours. Stir the beans a few times for the final 2 hours of cooking if possible.

3 Remove and discard bay leaf. Serve alongside rice.

PER SERVING
Calories: 499 | Fat: 10g | Protein: 33g | Sodium: 741mg | Fiber: 12g | Carbohydrates: 69g | Sugar: 3g

Tips, Substitutions, and More...

Dry pinto beans can be substituted for small red beans. Do *not* use dry kidney beans: They need to be boiled at least 10 minutes to kill off a naturally occurring toxic protein before cooking in a slow cooker so will not work for this recipe. Since all brands of creole seasoning are different, you may have to adjust the salt after cooking time is completed. Taste first and add salt slowly in 1/4 teaspoon increments.

Hoisin Pulled Pork Rice Bowls with Cucumbers

Combine a boneless pork butt with hoisin sauce, apple cider vinegar, and water, and set the slow cooker to cook all day. Later that evening, you have the most tender and flavorful pulled pork. Toss with a bit more hoisin and serve over rice alongside sliced cucumbers and kimchi for a dinner the whole family will crave time and time again.

PREP TIME: 5 MINUTES • ACTIVE COOK TIME: N/A • HANDS-OFF COOK TIME: 9 HOURS

1 (3$\frac{1}{2}$-pound) boneless Boston pork butt roast

1$\frac{1}{4}$ cups hoisin sauce, divided

$\frac{1}{4}$ cup apple cider vinegar

$\frac{1}{4}$ cup water

6 cups reheated precooked white rice

2 medium English cucumbers, sliced

1 cup kimchi

Tips, Substitutions, and More…

While the texture of shredded pork is recommended for this dish, you can use a chefs knife to cut sections into thin slices if you find that easier. Some additional toppings ideas include sliced scallions, toasted sesame seeds, sriracha, and shredded cabbage.

1 Combine pork roast, $\frac{1}{2}$ cup hoisin sauce, vinegar, and water in the insert of a 6-quart or larger slow cooker. Cover with lid and set to low for 9 hours.

2 Once cooking time is up, remove pork roast to a cutting board. Use two forks to shred and transfer to a large mixing bowl.

3 Reserve $\frac{1}{4}$ cup of cooking liquid, then discard remaining liquid so that slow cooker is empty. Return shredded pork, reserved cooking liquid, and remaining $\frac{3}{4}$ cup hoisin sauce to slow cooker. Toss until well combined.

4 Serve over rice alongside cucumbers and kimchi.

PER SERVING
Calories: 620 | Fat: 16g | Protein: 43g | Sodium: 876mg | Fiber: 1g | Carbohydrates: 76g | Sugar: 18g

Shortcut Ropa Vieja with Rice and Black Beans

SERVES
8

Inspired by the rich flavors of the Cuban dish ropa vieja, this shortcut version is effortlessly prepared in the slow cooker for a convenient twist on the beloved classic. Served over a bed of warm rice along with a pile of black beans and topped with chopped cilantro, this is a satisfying meal made with minimal effort.

PREP TIME: 10 MINUTES • ACTIVE COOK TIME: N/A • HANDS-OFF COOK TIME: 9½ HOURS

1 (28-ounce) can diced no-salt tomatoes

1/2 cup water

2 teaspoons dried oregano

2 teaspoons ground cumin

2 1/2 teaspoons kosher salt, divided

4 cloves garlic, peeled and crushed

1 medium yellow onion, peeled, halved, and thinly sliced

1 small jalapeño, seeded and thinly sliced

2 pounds flank steak, patted dry

1 teaspoon ground black pepper

8 ounces frozen mixed bell pepper strips

1/2 cup pitted small Manzanilla green olives with pimento, drained

2 tablespoons capers, drained

6 cups reheated precooked white rice

2 (15-ounce) cans black beans, drained, rinsed, and warmed

1/2 cup finely chopped fresh cilantro leaves

1 In the insert of a 6-quart or larger slow cooker, combine tomatoes, water, oregano, cumin, 1/2 teaspoon salt, garlic, onion, and jalapeño.

2 Place steak on a cutting board and rub both sides with remaining 2 teaspoons salt and black pepper until well coated. Use a sharp knife to slice steak into large sections (about four to six sections for a 2-pound flank steak), and place steak sections in slow cooker, burying under tomato mixture so that most of steak is submerged.

3 Cover with lid and set to low for 9 1/2 hours. After 9 hours of cooking time, remove steak to a cutting board.

4 Stir bell pepper, olives, and capers into sauce in slow cooker and replace lid.

5 Use two forks to shred steak. Return shredded steak to slow cooker, replace lid, and continue cooking for remaining cooking time (about 20 minutes).

6 Serve over rice and beans, topped with cilantro.

PER SERVING
Calories: 639 | Fat: 11g | Protein: 39g | Sodium: 1,742mg | Fiber: 13g | Carbohydrates: 96g | Sugar: 7g

Honey Balsamic Beef Stew with Crusty Bread

SERVES 6

This slow cooker Honey Balsamic Beef Stew is the perfect combination of savory and sweet. Loaded with chunks of potatoes, carrots, sliced mushrooms, and peas, this comforting and satisfying meal in a bowl will have everyone reaching for seconds. Serve with crusty bread.

PREP TIME: 10 MINUTES ● ACTIVE COOK TIME: N/A ● HANDS-OFF COOK TIME: 8 HOURS 15 MINUTES

2 pounds beef stew meat, cut into 1" cubes

1/3 cup all-purpose flour

1 tablespoon plus 2 teaspoons kosher salt

1/2 teaspoon ground black pepper

1/2 teaspoon dried thyme

1/2 cup low-sodium beef broth

1/4 cup balsamic vinegar

1/4 cup honey

2 tablespoons tomato paste

1 1/2 pounds Yukon Gold potatoes, unpeeled and cut into 1" chunks

3 medium carrots, scrubbed and cut into 1" chunks

1 large yellow onion, peeled, quartered, and thinly sliced

1 (10-ounce) package sliced white mushrooms

1 cup frozen peas

1 (12-ounce) crusty baguette, sliced

1. In the insert of a 6-quart or larger slow cooker, combine beef with flour, salt, pepper, and thyme until most of the flour is coating the beef.

2. Add broth, vinegar, honey, and tomato paste. Stir until mixed well with beef and any remaining flour. Add potato and carrot and stir to combine so that all of the beef cubes, potato pieces, and carrot chunks are submerged.

3. Top with onion and mushrooms and push down. Cover with lid and set to low for 8 hours. Stir one or two times during the last 2 hours of cooking if possible.

4. When cooking time is up, remove lid and add peas. Stir to mix in, then allow beef stew to sit without the lid 10–15 minutes to cool slightly, thicken sauce, and warm peas. Serve with sliced baguette.

PER SERVING
Calories: 774 | Fat: 28g | Protein: 48g | Sodium: 2,046mg | Fiber: 7g | Carbohydrates: 82g | Sugar: 18g

Tips, Substitutions, and More...

If you have organic carrots and they aren't particularly gritty, save even more time by skipping peeling and just give them a good scrub. Alternatively, you can swap in baby carrots. Low-sodium chicken broth can be substituted for beef broth. Feel free to garnish with fresh chopped parsley.

Mississippi-Style Pot Roast Sandwiches

SERVES
6

Get ready for a flavor-packed, fuss-free meal for a crowd. Tender pot roast is slow cooked to perfection in a simple mix of spices, pepperoncini, and broth. Pile the tender, shredded goodness onto sandwiches, throw some provolone cheese on top, and dinner is done—delicious and stress-free.

PREP TIME: 5 MINUTES • ACTIVE COOK TIME: N/A • HANDS-OFF COOK TIME: 8 HOURS

1 cup low-sodium beef broth

1 (12-ounce) jar pepperoncini, with juice, 6 whole pepperoncini reserved for serving

1½ tablespoons kosher salt

1 teaspoon ground black pepper

1 teaspoon garlic powder

1 teaspoon onion powder

1 teaspoon dried dill

1 teaspoon dried parsley

1 teaspoon dried chives

1 (3-pound) beef chuck roast

¼ cup salted butter, sliced into chunks

12 (1-ounce) slices provolone cheese

6 (6") soft white sandwich rolls

1 In the insert of a 6-quart or larger slow cooker, combine broth, pepperoncini (minus 6 set aside for serving) and juice, and spices. Add beef and top with butter. Cover with lid and set to low for 8 hours.

2 When cooking time is up, remove beef to a cutting board and use two forks to shred beef, then return to juice. On the same cutting board, thinly slice remaining pepperoncini for serving.

3 Add 2 slices provolone to each roll, only on top half of bread, leaving bottom free to soak up some juices. Add shredded beef and sliced pepperoncini, close sandwiches, and serve immediately.

PER SERVING
Calories: 827 | Fat: 47g | Protein: 62g | Sodium: 2,243mg | Fiber: 5g | Carbohydrates: 37g | Sugar: 1g

Tips, Substitutions, and More...

Not in the mood for sandwiches? Switch things up and serve over mashed potatoes with a side of a quick-cooking vegetable like snap peas or frozen peas. Save time by substituting 1 packet of high-quality ranch seasoning mix like Simply Organic for the spices. Be sure to taste the broth before adding the meat and add salt and pepper as needed.

FIND RECIPES FAST

Pressed for time? This section has you covered! Here you'll find lists of the recipes in this book with 5 minutes or less of prep time, 10 minutes or less of prep time, no active cooking time, and a total time to the table of 20 minutes or less.

Recipes with Prep Time of 5 Minutes or Less

Continued ▶

Recipes with Prep Time of 10 Minutes or Less

Recipes with No Active Cooking Time

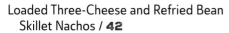

Continued ▶

Recipes with a Total Time to the Table of 20 Minutes or Less

Creamy Sun-Dried Tomato, Shrimp, and Gnocchi Skillet / **35**

Avocado Black Bean Quesadillas with Spicy Jack Cheese / **37**

Shredded Chicken Chilaquiles Verde / **47**

Italian Sausage and White Bean Skillet with Tortellini / **49**

5-Ingredient Authentic Fettuccine Alfredo / **53**

Shortcut Shakshuka with Feta / **56**

Panzanella Salad with Tuna and Fresh Mozzarella / **73**

Greek-Inspired Chickpea Salad with Pita Bread / **74**

Speedy Pesto Salmon and White Bean Lettuce Wraps / **76**

Peanut Sauce Chicken and Cabbage Bowls / **77**

Rotisserie Chicken Caprese Salad / **79**

Focaccia with Smoked Turkey and Garlicky Creole Mayo / **80**

Chopped Italian Sub Bowl / **83**

Za'atar-Spiced Chicken Salad Pita Pockets / **84**

Cheesy Baked Refried Bean Tacos / **105**

Taco Salmon with Avocado Lime Mash and Grilled Tomatoes / **123**

Adobo Swordfish with Pico de Gallo and Broccolini / **128**

Barbecue Cheddar Burgers with Quick Pickled Onions / **133**

One Pot Angel Hair Pasta with Crabmeat and Chives / **161**

Spicy Thai Green Curry Shrimp with Vegetables / **167**

Creamy Tortellini Soup with Ground Beef / **175**

15-Minute Coconut Curry Noodle Soup with Shrimp / **179**

Shortcut Vegetable Lo Mein / **180**

Ground Beef Stir-Fry with Bean Sprouts and Scallions / **184**

Thai Red Curry Pork Stir-Fry with Green Beans / **186**

Kimchi Beef Stir-Fry with Water Chestnuts / **189**

Copycat Chicken Lettuce Wraps / **190**

Super Quick Beef and Broccoli / **191**

US/METRIC CONVERSION CHART

OVEN TEMPERATURE CONVERSIONS

Degrees Fahrenheit	Degrees Celsius
200 degrees F	95 degrees C
250 degrees F	120 degrees C
275 degrees F	135 degrees C
300 degrees F	150 degrees C
325 degrees F	160 degrees C
350 degrees F	180 degrees C
375 degrees F	190 degrees C
400 degrees F	205 degrees C
425 degrees F	220 degrees C
450 degrees F	230 degrees C

BAKING PAN SIZES

American	Metric
8 × 1½ inch round baking pan	20 × 4 cm cake tin
9 × 1½ inch round baking pan	23 × 3.5 cm cake tin
11 × 7 × 1½ inch baking pan	28 × 18 × 4 cm baking tin
13 × 9 × 2 inch baking pan	30 × 20 × 5 cm baking tin
2 quart rectangular baking dish	30 × 20 × 3 cm baking tin
15 × 10 × 2 inch baking pan	30 × 25 × 2 cm baking tin (Swiss roll tin)
9 inch pie plate	22 × 4 or 23 × 4 cm pie plate
7 or 8 inch springform pan	18 or 20 cm springform or loose bottom cake tin
9 × 5 × 3 inch loaf pan	23 × 13 × 7 cm or 2 lb narrow loaf or pate tin
1½ quart casserole	1.5 liter casserole
2 quart casserole	2 liter casserole

WEIGHT CONVERSIONS

US Weight Measure	Metric Equivalent
1/2 ounce	15 grams
1 ounce	30 grams
2 ounces	60 grams
3 ounces	85 grams
1/4 pound (4 ounces)	115 grams
1/2 pound (8 ounces)	225 grams
3/4 pound (12 ounces)	340 grams
1 pound (16 ounces)	454 grams

VOLUME CONVERSIONS

US Volume Measure	Metric Equivalent
1/8 teaspoon	0.5 milliliter
1/4 teaspoon	1 milliliter
1/2 teaspoon	2 milliliters
1 teaspoon	5 milliliters
1/2 tablespoon	7 milliliters
1 tablespoon (3 teaspoons)	15 milliliters
2 tablespoons (1 fluid ounce)	30 milliliters
1/4 cup (4 tablespoons)	60 milliliters
1/3 cup	90 milliliters
1/2 cup (4 fluid ounces)	125 milliliters
2/3 cup	160 milliliters
3/4 cup (6 fluid ounces)	180 milliliters
1 cup (16 tablespoons)	250 milliliters
1 pint (2 cups)	500 milliliters
1 quart (4 cups)	1 liter (about)

INDEX

ABOUT ALYSSA BRANTLEY

Alyssa Brantley is the author of *The "I Don't Want to Cook" Book: 100 Tasty, Healthy, Low-Prep Recipes for When You Just Don't Want to Cook* and the creator of the popular recipe website EverydayMaven.com, where she shares seasonal recipes built on real food ingredients. Her motto is "Whole Food. Half the Time." Alyssa deeply believes that just because we are busy doesn't mean we shouldn't eat great!

In addition to sharing her kitchen creations, Alyssa is a food writer, food photographer, and food stylist.

Alyssa was raised in Philadelphia and now resides in Seattle with her husband and two sons. Having grown up in a cooking family, Alyssa learned to love food and explore flavors, cuisines, and ingredients from a very young age.

While living in New York City for college, Alyssa was an intern at the Food Network. During graduate school, she started a successful corporate lunch catering business called Grub Catering. She launched *EverydayMaven* after the birth of her first son, when she was looking for a creative outlet and began sharing the recipes she was using to lose extra pregnancy weight.

When Alyssa is not getting creative in the kitchen, she loves traveling, especially exploring new cities by walking and eating; spending time with her family; reading; and drinking wine on a sandy beach.

Her recipes and food photography have been featured by *People*, *Real Simple*, *Clean Eating*, *Gourmet*, *Shape*, *Self*, *Prevention*, *Parade*, *Redbook*, *HuffPost*, *BuzzFeed*, Today.com, and more.

ACKNOWLEDGMENTS

Thank you to my husband, Kareem, and our sons, Deacon and Vaughn, for always supporting my dreams, pushing me to be a better version of myself every day, and for patiently taste-testing hundreds of recipes—many that weren't necessarily your jam.

To my parents, for instilling in me the lesson that sitting down for family dinner most nights of the week is important, and for always having a table big enough to welcome hungry friends and family. To my brother, Adam; to Debbie; and to all of my extended family and friends—I wish my campaign to have all of you move to Seattle was more successful. Life is more fun when we are together.

To my meme squad; you know who you are. I am convinced that is what the Internet was invented for. Daily laughter is key; thank you for making sure I don't take myself too seriously.

To all of my supporters—to my website readers, everyone who bought my first book, and everyone who cooks any of my recipes. It brings me so much joy to receive messages from people around the world who have stories to tell about how one of my website or book recipes has become a family tradition, has helped them win a chili cook-off, or has made their child love a new food. This is absolutely the best thing ever. So, thank you a million times!!!

I'm forever grateful to have these platforms to share food creations and be continually inspired and challenged to try new ideas, new techniques, and new flavor combinations.

To everyone at Simon & Schuster and Adams Media for making this project happen—and continuing the "I Don't Want to Cook" series.

Delicious and nutritious recipes —without the hard work!

100 TASTY, HEALTHY, LOW-PREP RECIPES for When You Just DON'T Want to Cook

THE "I DON'T WANT TO COOK" BOOK

ALYSSA BRANTLEY
FOUNDER OF EVERYDAYMAVEN

Pick up or download your copy today!